# *Beauty* for Ashes Vol. 1

## Transforming Testimonies for Every Woman

Juanita R. Ingram, Esq.

WestBow
PRESS
A DIVISION OF THOMAS NELSON

Scriptures taken from the Holy Bible, New International Version®, NIV®. Copyright © 1973, 1978, 1984, 2011 by Biblica, Inc.™ Used by permission of Zondervan. All rights reserved worldwide. www.zondervan.com

The "NIV" and "New International Version" are trademarks registered in the United States Patent and Trademark Office by Biblica, Inc.™

Scripture taken from the King James Version of the Bible.

WestBow Press books may be ordered through booksellers or by contacting:

WestBow Press
A Division of Thomas Nelson
1663 Liberty Drive
Bloomington, IN 47403
www.westbowpress.com
1 (866) 928-1240

ISBN: 978-1-4908-1571-8 (sc)
ISBN: 978-1-4908-1572-5 (e)

Library of Congress Control Number: 2013921092

Printed in the United States of America.

WestBow Press rev. date: 11/18/2013

# Contents

Testimony 1 ............................................................................1
Sherry's Testimony

Testimony 2 ............................................................................8
Kimmerly's Testimony

Testimony 3 ..........................................................................17
Rebecca's Testimony

Testimony 4 ..........................................................................23
Nieika's Testimony

Testimony 5 ..........................................................................28
Jonique's Testimony

Testimony 6 ..........................................................................31
Jurrita's Testimony

Testimony 7 ..........................................................................34
Juanita's Testimony

Testimony 8 ..........................................................................42
Neysa's Testimony

Testimony 9 ..........................................................................45
Joyce's Testimony

Testimony 10 ........................................................................48
Valerie's Testimony

Testimony 11......................................................51
Anonymous Testimony

Testimony 12 ....................................................56
ShaQuita's Testimony

Testimony 13 ....................................................60
Tifinie's Testimony

Testimony 14......................................................65
Alicia's Testimony

Testimony 15......................................................70
Noma's Testimony

Testimony 16......................................................74
Anonymous Testimony

Testimony 17......................................................76
Anonymous Testimony

# Subject Matter Appendix

**Abuse**

        Testimony 3

        Testimony 10

        Testimony 12

**Bullying**

        Testimony 3

**Business Advice/ Entrepreneurship**

        Testimony 14

**Children with Special Needs**

        Testimony 5

**Confidence/Self-Esteem**

        Testimony 2

        Testimony 13

        Testimony 15

**Consequences of Sin**

        Testimony 2

**Dating/ Purity**

        Testimony 3

        Testimony 2

        Testimony 13

**Dealing with Offense/ Deceit**

        Testimony 17

        Testimony 8

**Death**

        Testimony 1

**Deliverance**

        Testimony 2

        Testimony 3

        Testimony 10

**Developing a Relationship with God**

        Testimony 2

        Testimony 3

        Testimony 6

**Encouragement**

        Testimony 1

        Testimony 4

        Testimony 14

        Testimony 15

**Forgiveness**

        Testimony 1

        Testimony 17

        Testimony 8

        Testimony 10

**Fornication**

        Testimony 2

        Testimony 8

**Friendship**

        Testimony 3

**Healing (Physically)**

        Testimony 4

        Testimony 7

**Healing after Abortion**

        Testimony 2

**Health and Fitness**

        Testimony 4
        Testimony 15

**Infidelity**

        Testimony 8

**Job Satisfaction**

        Testimony 16

**Loneliness**

        Testimony 2
        Testimony 3
        Testimony 6
        Testimony 13

**Marriage**

        Testimony 3
        Testimony 5
        Testimony 8
        Testimony 13

**Miscarriage**

        Testimony 5

**Multi-Cultural Marriage**

        Testimony 3

**Overcoming Societal Stigma**

        Testimony 3
        Testimony 4
        Testimony 11

**Perseverance/Faith**

Testimony 1
Testimony 9
Testimony 12

**Purpose**

Testimony 1
Testimony 2
Testimony 4
Testimony 5
Testimony 15

**Salvation**

Testimony 2
Testimony 3
Testimony 5

**Suicide**

Testimony 1
Testimony 2

**Temptation**

Testimony 2

**Waiting on God-sent Love**

Testimony 3
Testimony 6
Testimony 13
Testimony 11

**Witnessing**

Testimony 3

# Dedication

I dedicate this book to the Lord.

May this work Glorify You and Your perfect will be done.

Amen.

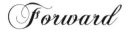

# Forward

**Revelation 12:11 "And they overcame him by the blood of the Lamb, _and by the word of their testimony_; and they loved not their lives unto the death." (KJV)**

I would like to thank God for allowing me the privilege to share the testimonies that are contained in this book. It is beyond an honor and a privilege to be able to help spread these testimonies to the masses, encouraging women across the world to trust God with their problems, issues, and dreams. I would like to express my deepest level of appreciation and gratitude to the women who submitted their testimony in the desire to inspire, encourage, and equip other women to live victorious lives through Christ.

One of the most powerful tools to transform the lives of others from a place of defeat to a place of victory is through the Word of God, the blood of the Lamb and the power of our testimonies. Our testimony is not the doctrine we simply commit to memory and give to others. It is the very life that we live as witnessed by Jesus himself! Our testimony is the evidence of the glory of Christ that we offer to the world!

Within the pages of this book are testimonies that address real issues – issues that may be present in your life; which are discussed with transparency, honesty and truthfulness. The Bible says in James 5:16 _"Confess your faults one to another, and pray one for another, that ye may be healed. The effectual fervent prayer of a righteous man availeth much."_ (KJV). Transforming ministry is truly born out of the weaknesses that we continually expose and confess. The confession that one struggles with depression, or is addicted to drugs, or struggles with fornication is not a negative declaration. When this action of confession is incorporated with repentance, righteous prayer, and accountability, then the power of God's divine healing will flow!

In Isaiah 61:1-3 God declares that He will give you beauty for your ashes. Trust and believe that He is going to take your difficult, discouraging, horrific, hurtful, and depressing situation and give you beauty. He will pull you up out of life's pile of ashes and make something beautiful out of you and your situation – just as He has in the lives of the women who shared their testimonies in the book.

I pray that as you continue to read this book the Holy Spirit will move and each testimony will aid you in your own transformation.

Amen.

Selah.

### Isaiah 61:1-3 (NIV)
### The Year of the Lord's Favor

1 The Spirit of the Sovereign Lord is on me,
because the Lord has anointed me
to preach good news to the poor.
He has sent me to bind up the brokenhearted,
to proclaim freedom for the captives
and release from darkness for the prisoners,
2 to proclaim the year of the Lord's favor
and the day of vengeance of our God,
to comfort all who mourn,
3 and provide for those who grieve in Zion—
to bestow on them a crown of beauty
instead of ashes, the oil of gladness
instead of mourning, and a garment of praise
instead of a spirit of despair.
They will be called oaks of righteousness,
a planting of the Lord
for the display of his splendor.

# Testimony 1

## By Sherry Westland

### "Rebuilt by Brokenness"

It has been said that what does not kill you makes you stronger. That is true, yet I have discovered that there is more to that saying. Allow me to share my story of blessing, tragedy, and hope.

I was blessed with three wonderful sons. Today, I want you to get to know my oldest son, Ryan. We were very close. He once said, "If I could choose any mom in the world, I would choose you." I was truly blessed by this young man. He was full of love and laughter. You would have loved him too; everyone who knew him did. Many mothers wanted him for their son-in-law. He was not afraid to show affection. He was definitely a people person.

Ryan loved to make others laugh, and he played lots of practical jokes. For instance, I had not worked at my husband's CPA firm very long when Ryan called me and pretended to be a farmer. Living in Minnesota, we have some clients who are farmers. Using his best accent, Ryan proceeded to tell me he had "Plum forgot about doing his taxes and wondered if he could pop in without an appointment." I was thinking, "Is this Ryan?", so I asked him his address. He had done his homework because he gave me a legitimate address in our area. I said, "Sure, you can come by." He proceeded to say, "Well, Ma'am, I'm sorry to tell ya that I'm wearing my overalls and they're pretty dirty. There's no time to change, and I'm kinda smelly. Is that okay?" I was giggling to myself and assured him it would be okay. All of a sudden, he yelled, "Whoooo-eeeeeee, my prize pig just escaped! I'll have to call you back!" He waited a couple of hours before he called back and started over with his accent, only to burst out laughing and say, "Gotcha!" His call brought some much-needed levity to an otherwise stressful day. Yes, that was my son.

Ryan used to call me from California almost daily and we would talk about everything. He would always end the conversation with, "I love you mom." I would tell him how much he was loved. We were a joy to one another.

When Ryan loved, he loved without reserve—with his whole heart. He was madly in love with a young woman who had two children. He loved her children as his own, and they loved him as a father. He had just turned 31 and planned to marry her and adopt her children. He was excited when she flew out to California, because he planned to surprise her with a proposal and an engagement ring. However, he was blindsided and crushed when she broke up with him instead.

After this incident, he stopped calling me frequently. He withdrew from everyone. I was concerned, but knew he was working things out and probably needed some space. I finally called him a few weeks later. He was different, disconnected. I did not know what to do or say. I told him I missed that guy who used to call me. Then he started calling me more frequently, but if he did not think he had my full attention, it made him agitated. I was confused, as I had never seen him act that way. I felt it was still due to him working through his break-up, so I gave him space.

Ryan did not show up for work on Tuesday morning, May 11. My youngest son, Keith, called from California asking if I had heard from him. Ryan NEVER missed work. He had a wonderful job with Southern California Edison. He was a very hard worker. I knew something was very wrong. I started praying and hoping that somehow, he was safe. In the midst of my panic, I felt God's presence and peace come over me. It was not so much knowing that Ryan was still alive, but feeling the power of God's presence. Hours later, it was confirmed that the unthinkable had happened. Ryan intentionally overdosed, numbing his pain with both alcohol and pain killers (which had a side effect of suicidal thoughts). This act forever changed my life and the lives of all who loved him.

My precious son took his life on Monday, May 10, 2011. The last time I talked to him was the day before—on Mother's Day. I knew he was feeling down, and I tried to encourage him. He responded with, "Maybe that is the answer." I knew he was searching for answers, and I hoped I had given him some positive ideas to ponder.

Ryan had struggled with depression off and on over the years, which I believe was due to an unresolved tragedy he experienced shortly after graduating high school. He would never let anyone help him sort through it. He did not like to talk about it, and he kept his feelings buried inside. I believe it was this unresolved issue, complicated and triggered by the break-up, which caused him to take his life. It sent him into a tailspin from which he never recovered. He had reached his threshold of pain and had believed Satan's lies that he should give up hope.

I will never forget when I got the call that Ryan was gone. Words cannot express the grief that comes with the loss of a loved one, perhaps more so with the loss of a child. Humanly speaking, shock actually helped me to get through the initial weeks after my loss. I remember thinking that things would get better in time, yet, I did not realize the daily waves of grief that come after the shock wears off.

I really needed to hear from God directly. My daily worship felt like a one-way communication, perhaps because I was such an emotional wreck. I needed God's grace and mercy to take over. I will always remember the morning I drove alone to Minneapolis for a meeting. I left very early, and I talked with God the whole way. It was my day for a breakthrough as I felt God's assurance that I would see my son again, and that Ryan was safe in God's care. It was one of those "God things", when you know you have spent time in the presence of the true and living God. It was healing to hear His soft voice and know that He cared enough to touch me personally. It brought hope to my innermost being. God is close to the broken hearted; on that you can believe.

It was a blessing to feel the love shown by friends during the early weeks. They cried with me, gave much-needed hugs and gifts of love. They helped ease my heavy load, because the burden was too heavy to carry on my own. God was at work through my friends. 2 Corinthians 1:3-4 says, *"Praise be to the God and Father of our Lord Jesus Christ, the Father of compassion and the God of all comfort, who comforts us in all our troubles, so that we can comfort those in any trouble with the comfort we ourselves receive from God."* (NIV) I praise God for his foreknowledge of knowing how to meet us in our need, working through the hands and feet of others.

Still, as the months dragged on, life for me became a chore. I had lost my energy and my fun-loving spirit. I did not want to do much of anything. It has been two years now, and I still struggle, because I miss him so much, yet God is so good. Although it still hurts deeply, I see progress with purpose. On my bad days, I pray and talk with God and with Ryan. I imagine what Ryan would say to me, because I know he would not want me to remain pitiful. I have found this three-way communion to help me heal. God has used these conversations to lift my head on those dark days.

I still go over the events leading to my son's death. Looking back, we could piece together the warning signs and verbal clues that Ryan was not doing well. The weekend before, he had talked to his friends about taking his life. He sent a text to another friend saying that he would not be around much longer, yet no one knew how to respond. We were all concerned, but did not want to believe he would really do it. He had reached his threshold, and even though he did not really want to die, he was clinically depressed and could not see any other way out of his pain.

Since his death, I have learned some things I did not know about my son. I knew he freely loved and laughed, however, I did not know how much his friends depended on him to encourage and support them. I have heard numerous stories of the love and encouragement he gave to his friends. I am so proud of the man he was and the legacy he left behind for us to remember.

Since the Bible tells us that our days are numbered, I ask, "What can I do with my days to help my tragedy not become someone else's tragedy?" God has given me the answer. Knowledge is power, and I started by becoming QPR certified to help prevent suicide. Now I know what could have potentially been done to save Ryan's life, but there is no power in the past—only in the present. There are no second chances for Ryan, but there are second chances for the living. God has given me the opportunity to do in the present what I desperately wished for in the past. God took my worst tragedy and added his best to it. What the devil meant for harm, God has turned around for good. He is rebuilding my life by my brokenness, so that I can make a difference.

As I have faced the facts, accepted them, let go and let God, He has turned my tragedy into something that can help save others. Out of my greatest tragedy, my life purpose was born. I have become an advocate for suicide prevention, focusing on public awareness, education, and resources—all to the glory of God. God truly is giving me "beauty for ashes."

Perhaps you, too, have lost a loved one, and you realize you cannot fix the situation by yourself. Be assured that we can fix our minds on the God who is able. We are not promised a problem-free life, but God assures us that there is no storm too great. Hebrews 4:16 says, "Let us then approach God's throne of grace with confidence, so that we may receive mercy and find grace to help us in our time of need."

The important thing in life is not so much that we begin well, or even how well we navigate our journey. The important thing is that we end well, so that we contribute something and make the world a better place for those who come after us. My son's life was filled with love and laughter. He reminds me to love and laugh more often.

As a suicide survivor (one who has lost a loved one to suicide), I have found God's grace, mercy, and strength to be enough for me. God has used my worst tragedy to shape my life, and to deepen my love for Him and others. He has given me empathy for the hurting. It is hard work to heal after the loss of a loved one. Some survivors find it hard to go on. If you are struggling to find meaning in life, and you wonder if it is worth it, let me say, "I have been where you are, and it changed me forever, but let me help you choose life again". God has a plan for your life. He wants to give you purpose.

Yes, God uses even the most painful moments in our lives to deepen our trust in Him and to give us more compassion for others who hurt as we do. God's plan to give hope and direction to those who struggle, involves ordinary people like me teaming up with an extraordinary God. He takes the pitiful and makes them powerful. The Holy Spirit gives grace that enables God's love to overflow into the lives of others. I am dedicated to sharing the hope and healing that is found in Christ. Today is a beautiful time for grace.

I cherish Ryan's memory, and I am so thankful to have had him for 31 years. The loss of a loved one is so tragic. I do not want others to go through what we have gone through. It is my passion to impart hope to the hopeless and to leave the world a better place than I found it. I am hopeful that one day the world will be rid of suicide entirely, as lies are replaced with truth and hope. All life is valuable and worth living. My son will be a memory in my heart forever. It is not what I wanted, but it is what it is. I long for the day when I will be with him again, when our Lord and Savior returns to restore everything to His original plan. The scripture I cling to is in Joel 2:25. "And *I will restore to you the years that the locust hath eaten...*" (KJV) Thank you, Lord, for this blessed hope.

Yes, what does not kill you makes you stronger, but it takes positive action. If someone you know is talking about committing suicide, please take them seriously. Intervene and get them help. I do not want my tragedy to become your tragedy. Please visit my website for resources to help the hopeless and hurting.

## AUTHOR BIOGRAPHY

Sherry lived most of her life in California, until she moved to Minnesota in 2006. Wife to Stan, a proud mother of two (living) sons, and two beautiful granddaughters, she loves her family and her God. She has been an avid scuba diver, which has taken her to many exotic destinations worldwide. Mrs. Westland has a varied background, primarily as a Flight Attendant, Certified Fitness Instructor, and Executive Assistant to a hospital CEO, having studied Business Administration in college.

She is currently an Office Manager for a CPA Firm and Conservator for her half sister's estate. She enjoys facilitating the Dare to Care Program at her church and is also a Truth Media online mentor. She was awarded a DTM from Toastmaster's International, as well as other Toastmaster leadership awards, and has received multiple Chairman's Awards for Service Excellence.

She is committed to being an advocate for suicide prevention, education, and awareness. Not wanting her tragedy to become another's tragedy, she is a QPR Certified Gatekeeper. Her hobbies include golf, fitness, reading, traveling, Vikings Football, and riding the Harley with her husband. Sherry is always stepping out of her comfort zone to see how God wants to use her in His service. She is the reigning Senior Ms. Global United International (Yes, there is such a pageant for senior women over 60, and, no, there is not a swimsuit competition) and will compete at the Ms. Senior America pageant in 2013.

## Testimony 2

# By Kimmerly Harrell

It is funny how God brings things full circle. Here it is 2013 and my life has made a 360 over the last 8 years. In 2005, you couldn't get me to believe that I would be sitting where I am today and headed in the direction I'm going. In 2005, at the age of 29, I had just graduated with my Master's degree in Communicative Disorders. My goal was to pass my certification exam and go on to get my PhD. I've always wanted to teach at the university level and do research and that was where I was headed…but, little did I know I would end up having an 8 year detour…

I grew up in the church and went every Sunday. My Grandfather was a Minister so we spent a lot of time in church. I always knew about God, but for a long time I didn't "know" God. As I grew into my teenage years, I was very promiscuous. I lost my virginity at age 15 and my life seemed to revolve around boys. As I got older, many of those relationships started to take a toll on me. I didn't realize I was looking for love and affection, I thought I was just having fun, fitting in, and following the crowd. But in actuality, the crowd wasn't doing all of these things. I remember I once had a friend in high school to tell me, "You don't have to do this stuff to get people to like you. We are your friends". But I was really a young girl with low self-esteem looking to be loved. As I went on to college, I started to have more "serious" monogamous relationships. I started to think about getting married, having a family, and etc. A couple of times during my promiscuous season of life I even contracted different STDs.

By the time I graduated from college and moved back to my hometown, I was exhausted from relationships and wanted something new. I started attending church and learning about what it is to actually know God and have a relationship with Him.

Relationship? With God? That was all new to me. I knew who God was and how He worked, but I didn't have an intimate relationship with Him. I met someone during this time and thought I had truly found love. We attended church together and Bible study. We prayed and studied the Word together. And after a while, we were sleeping together. That is when I learned what conviction was, that horrible feeling I had in my stomach after we had sex for the first time. But we didn't stop. Our relationship progressed and got more serious. And then, I became pregnant and it changed everything. I was excited about being a mother, but my partner wasn't and he demanded I have an abortion. I wanted to keep him in my life. He had already told me he wouldn't support me or be with me if I kept the baby. I wanted him in my life, so, on October 5, 2001, I did the unthinkable and aborted the child that was growing in me.

The emotional and physical effects were almost unbearable. Suicide crossed my mind so many times and once almost became a reality. Sadly, in the end, after years of multiple resuscitations, the relationship still did not survive. After the abortion, I attended a post-abortion Bible study for women. God really had to work on me because I harbored so much anger and unforgiveness towards myself and my boyfriend at the time. After our relationship ended, I continued to date other people and continued to have unsuccessful relationships.

Jumpstart to 2005. I've graduated and moved to Atlanta. My plan is to only stay in Atlanta for the summer because I'm leaving in the fall to start on my PhD. Well, our plans are not always God's plans. That "summer" turned into months, which turned into years. But it wasn't all bad.

I joined a wonderful church and got back on track with my relationship with God. I was so excited about where God was taking me. I never forgot my dream of going back to school, but I wanted God so much at that point that I was willing to wait as long as I had to. After a while, I met a young man at church. He was very interesting because he was everything that I had imagined I wanted my husband to be. He fit the profile 100%. He and I became very good friends and we were very close. We served in ministry together and prayed together. God even used him in a mighty way in my life. But once again, it ended up going in the wrong direction and God discontinued the relationship, but kept the friendship strong.

Over the next few years, I continued to grow my faith. I became more active in church and started to hear God clearly in my every day activities. But I also continued to fall in sin. I got involved in an affair with a married co-worker that ended up being very embarrassing and I ended up transferring jobs. I continued going to church, praying and being active. I also started writing and leading the young ladies in my youth group. I knew that God had given me a testimony that needed to get to young ladies. So many of them were dealing with the same issues I had dealt with: promiscuity, abortion, low self-esteem, STD's. God used my testimony to heal me also. I remember thinking how no man would ever want to be with me. But God drew my attention to His word in Isaiah 53: 5 "But he was pierced for our transgressions, he was crushed for our iniquities; the punishment that brought us peace was upon him, and by his wounds we are healed." I had to start believing God's word and believing that I was healed. I had to start walking in my healing, despite what the doctors and my body was telling me. I believed the Word of God. I knew God wanted to use me. But why? I was sleeping with a married man and still coming to church and serving like everything was okay. Why in the world would God want to use me for anything?

Once the affair ended and I moved to a different job, I started dating again. I desired to be celibate, but I wasn't getting involved with men who had the same desire, so I took a break from worldly dating and started putting all my energy into serving God. I spoke and gave my testimony to the young people, both male and female, in our youth group. I was so afraid of what they would say and what they would think about me in the end. But I had to look past all of that and focus on

God. I was doing what He called me to do and nothing else mattered. I started teaching in our church.

After a year or so of handling all of the administrative responsibility of our youth department, I found myself in a very compromising position. Even though I wasn't involved in a relationship with anyone, I was still dealing with sexual sin. I ended up being in the worst relationship I could have ever imagined; an affair with my youth Pastor. It all happened so quickly, but it was also very short lived. I remember just being numb at times and in a zombie state. I was a robot, doing my routine as usual on Thursday night during our youth services, ignoring the fact that I was sleeping with the youth Pastor. Our ministry was very close knit. We did many things together outside of church. I was close to our youth Pastor's wife and his children. Everything ended when someone, following the orders of God, intervened. And even though I was very bitter and angry towards this person, who was a very close friend of mine, I am so thankful to God that he was obedient.

The fall-out was devastating. I was seen as this woman who had bad motives. Many people called me a home wrecker and stopped speaking to me even to this day. In so many ways, I was cast-out from this church, the place that I loved and served with all my heart. I had hit rock bottom. A couple of weeks later, I gathered all the prescription drugs that I had left over from previous surgeries. I had numerous Vicodin and Percocet pills and had laid them all out on the table. I sat there and said "God, give me one good reason why I shouldn't take these?"

As I proceeded to open the bottles, someone knocked on my door. I wasn't expecting anybody and nobody knew I was getting ready to take my own life. At the door was a friend of mine, the same friend who had followed God's orders to intervene with the affair I was having with our youth Pastor. He had never been to my apartment before. The only thing he knew was the side of town I lived in. He got the manager at my apartment complex to bring him to my apartment. The manager was there with him and he was going to open the door if I hadn't answered. He told me that God had put me in his spirit all week long and he didn't know why. He said he prayed and prayed and God told him exactly how to get to my apartment. I saw God differently from that day on.

I always knew I had a purpose, but after that day, I knew without a shadow of a doubt that God loved me and had a plan so big for my life, that not even the devil himself would be able to stop it. At that moment, Jeremiah 15:19 became real, *"If you repent, I will restore you that you may serve me; if you utter worthy, not worthless words, you will be my spokesman..."* (NIV) I was going to have to take the precious from the vile. God was going to use that which was bad and make it good for His glory.

I had a long road ahead. I sought counseling from professionals and I also had to learn about who my friends really were. I started thinking about everything that had happened to me— the abortion, the affairs, the diseases, the failed relationships. I was trying to hold on to God's Word, but it was so hard. I felt isolated and alone. There are some days when I could not even get out of bed. I kept wishing I could go back and have a complete do-over of my life. I didn't have a church home anymore, so I visited a lot of churches. Every new church I visited I felt like everyone was staring at me and knew what I had done. I finally stopped going all together. I had to take my trust of God to a whole new level. I knew that God never waste a hurt. I knew He wanted to use all of my hurts for good, but I only saw myself as a broken, useless vessel. I had so many questions regarding my walk with God and what it truly, truly meant to be in relationship with Him and love Him. And little by little, my Father started to speak through His Word. On a daily basis I had to meditate on some on the Scriptures below, this is what kept me:

> Joel 2:25 I will repay you for the years the locusts have eaten... (NIV)

> Psalm 71:20 Though you have made me see troubles, many and bitter, you will restore my life again; from the depths of the earth you will again bring me up. (NIV)

> Romans 8:28 And we know that in all things God works for the good of those who love him, who have been called according to his purpose. (NIV)

Isaiah 43:18-19 Forget the former things; do not dwell on the past. See, I am doing a new thing. Now it springs up; do you not perceive it? I am making a way in the desert and streams in the wasteland. (NIV)

Isaiah 43:25 I, even I, am he who blots out your transgressions, for my own sake, and remembers your sins no more. (NIV)

I held on to every last word that God spoke to me. He was the only way I was going to be able to pull myself together. I had repented and I knew He had forgiven me. I eventually started attending church again, for a short while I even started going back to my former church. I had to get a better understanding of sin and why I was doing the things I had done. Sin separates us from God and with sin there is always a death. The youth ministry at my church had died because of my sin. A friend of mine once compared sin to "tonic immobility." Tonic immobility is described as a natural state of paralysis that animals enter. For example, a shark can be placed in a tonic immobility state by turning it upside down. The shark remains in this state of paralysis for an average of 15 minutes before it recovers. Sin can be like this. Our ability to honor God can be put in "tonic immobility" by the power and consequences of sin. God showed me I had been in a "tonic immobility" state for many years.

After a couple of years, I started focusing more on my career dreams. I still needed to pass my test for my certification license and I wanted to get my PhD. Standardized test have never been a strength of mine, but I was determined to make it happen. I went through several disappointments of not getting the test score I needed and getting rejected to PhD programs because of my low GRE scores. But God had put this desire in my heart and Psalm 37:4 said *"Delight yourself in the Lord, and he will give you the desires of your heart."* (English Standard Version) Psalm 37:7 says *"Be still before the Lord and wait patiently for him."* (NIV) I meditated on these Scriptures day and night. I knew God was going to allow me to pass my certification exam and get into a PhD program. I just didn't know when.

In the fall of 2011, I found out some crushing career news. My internship that I had completed in 2005 upon graduation was no longer valid because I did not pass my test and receive my certification within two years after graduating. Therefore, I would have to complete it again and pass my test before the certification standards changed in 2014. I was so disappointed, but I remembered God's Word and I knew He was not going to fail me, Luke 1:45 *"Blessed is she who has believed that what the Lord has said to her will be accomplished."* (NIV)

All of this meant I had to find another job and find someone to "supervise" me. Now, by this time, I had been a Speech-Language Pathologist going on seven years, I did not need supervision by far. But I had to humble myself and do what I needed to do. I ended up going to work for a travel company that moved me to Florida. I ended up taking around a $30,000 pay cut because I was now considered a "clinical intern". Once I got to Florida, I found a church to attend and I kept studying for my test and looking into PhD programs.

I had some programs flat out tell me I shouldn't even be thinking about PhD programs because I wasn't even certified. But I recalled what Habakkuk 2:2-3 says *"Write the vision and make it plain on tablets. That he may run who reads it. For the vision is yet for an appointed time; but at the end it will speak, and it will not lie. Though it tarries, wait for it; because it will surely come, it will not tarry."* (NKJV) I saw myself being a professor. On my notes and pieces of paper at work and at school, I would always scribble, Kimmerly Harrell, PhD, CCC-SLP. My password for my new job I started in 2012 was '2013phd!' I knew I was going to school in the fall of 2103 and I knew God had called me to be a fully licensed and certified Speech-Language Pathologist. He put that desire in my heart and He was going to bring it to pass.

January 2013, I went to take my certification exam, just as I had done 14 times previously over the last eight years. But this time was different. As I sat there and took my test, I felt a presence of peace come over me that was so strong, so undeniable. I walked out and knew deep down, like never before in the past, that I had passed my test. And in February, God confirmed it! In March, He then confirmed my other dream. I was accepted into the PhD program I applied to! For a couple of weeks I was so overcome by emotions. I was praising and thanking God. Numbers 23:19 says *"God is not a man, that he should lie, not a human being, that he should change his mind. Does he speak and then not act? Does he promise and not fulfill?"* (NIV)

As the weeks went on, God started to speak and reveal some things to me. He showed me how it had been eight years from the time I graduated (2005) and had so many things happen, until now, 2013. In Biblical numerology, eight is the number of new beginnings. God told me that 2013 is my year of new beginnings and everything that has happened that was supposed to destroy me, He will now use it for His good and glory. On the same day I found out I had passed my test, my devotional from Joel Osteen for that day said "You need to get ready; not for a trickle, not a stream, but a flood of God's favor, a tidal wave of God's goodness." In 2005, was when I was first truly on fire for God, it's when I started writing, started giving my testimony to young girls, and when I truly understood what God had called me to do. Today, in 2013, I believe God is giving me a rebirth and bringing all of those things back with a greater anointing than in 2005.

There is nothing that God cannot do. And there is nothing that we can ever do for Him to not love us. God desires to redeem and restore the broken. I had to learn that my heart was the key to devotion to God. Jeremiah 29:13 says *"You will seek me and find me when you seek me with all your heart."* (NIV) And even though, God has brought all of my dreams and desires to pass, I am still, and I will constantly seek Him. I've rededicated myself to staying pure until I get married. I want to love, honor, and obey God. I believe in God's promises. I have heard them, read them, and seen them come to pass. The great thing is that He wants to give all of His children the desires of their hearts, but we have to love and obey Him. John 14:15 says it clear and plain *"If you love me, you will obey what I command."* (NIV)

Years ago while going through the post-abortion Bible study for women, we studied and meditated on numerous Scriptures. But the very first one we studied and talked about was Isaiah 61:1-3, *"The Spirit of the Sovereign Lord is on me, because the Lord has anointed me to preach good news to the poor. He has sent me to bind up the brokenhearted, to proclaim freedom for the captives and release from darkness for the prisoners, to proclaim the year of the Lord's favor and the day of vengeance of our God to comfort all who mourn, and provide for those who grieve in Zion-to bestow on them a crown of beauty instead of ashes, the oil of gladness instead of mourning, and a garment of praise instead of a spirit of despair. They will be called oaks of righteousness, a planting of the Lord for the display of his splendor."* (NIV) I remember crying uncontrollably during this first session when she read this Scripture, and I couldn't understand why at the time. Three months later, when our Bible study had ended and we had our memorial service for our unborn children, they read this same Scripture again, but I didn't cry this time. I smiled and had so much peace because I understood what it meant and what God was going to do for me and for millions of other women. And even today, He wants to give His daughters beauty for their ashes, praise, instead of despair.

## AUTHOR BIOGRAPHY

 Kimmerly K. Harrell was born and raised in the South. She grew up between Tennessee and Mississippi and has also lived in Georgia. She currently resides in Ocala, Florida. She earned her B.S. from Tennessee State University, her M.S. from the University of Mississippi, and her EdS from Lincoln Memorial University. She is a licensed Speech-Language Pathologist who has worked with adults and children, but specializes in language and literacy disorders. She currently works as a travel therapist, but beginning in August 2013, she will be a full-time PhD student at the University of Central Florida in Orlando, Florida.

# TESTIMONY 3

## By Rebecca Cheung Kallioniemi

People see me with a wonderful husband and a successful career. They tell me I am tall and pretty. They see how my life is now and think I have always been so blessed, but that is far from the truth. Please allow me to share the story of how God took my ashes and turned them into a life of beauty.

I was born out of wedlock, which was a mark of shame in my Asian culture. When my mom was between six and seven months pregnant, she went to the temple to find out my gender. She was told that I was a boy, which made her very happy, but then they told her that she would die in childbirth. Her fear led her to ask for an abortion, but she was too far along for that.

Later, my mom discovered that my father was leading a double life. He had a wife and children in Singapore, too. My mom wanted to give me to the other family in Singapore. To add complication to my already complicated family life, my dad died when I was five years old, and then my mom wanted to send me to an orphanage. I continued to live with her, but she was always angry and abusive.

As a child, I had attention deficit problems. I was very hyperactive as well. Because I was so outspoken and hyper, it made school difficult. I attended a Catholic school, where I was quickly labeled as a problem child by the harsh and unloving teachers. I was always blamed for any problems that arose in the classroom. The teachers actually told the other children to avoid me and gave them permission to slap me in the face. I had no friends, which caused me to become very lonely and defensive.

During my childhood, I was bounced around among my family, which led to me being sexually abused as a small girl. My mom drank and beat me all the time. I learned to comfort myself by watching programs about nice families on television. In my room at night, I would use dolls to act out plays in which I was loved and accepted by my family. My grandmother was a Christian, and she loved and prayed for me, but she died when I was only 14 years old. The rest of my family considered me a burden. They were always ashamed of the fact that I was born out of wedlock.

At 15 years old, I was sent to live with my uncle in Canada, but I did not get along well with him, so I was sent to a boarding school. Because the school was expensive, I was sent back to Hong Kong within a year. While I was in high school, my half-sister came to live with us. She worked and was the main breadwinner for my family, which she resented. This caused tension in our family.

When I was 16 and a half, my mom wanted me to become a model. She wanted me to become successful and bring riches and glamour to our lives. I became a model and started hanging out with celebrities, but my relationships with these people was not sincere. I became paranoid about losing friends. During this time, I went through several short relationships with boys. When I was 19, a man seduced me and took my virginity.

When I was 20 and a half, my mom got married for the third time. She was very domineering over her new husband. He became a "yes man" to keep the peace. I soon moved back to Canada to get away from my mom. I went back to school and finished my high school education. After that, I began to attend a university. I was able to make some friends, but we wanted to party all the time.

My mom had always been superstitious, but then she got involved in Buddhism and fortune telling. This was around the time that I was almost ready to graduate from the university. My mom was a carrier of Hepatitis B, so she regularly had tests and scans of her liver to make sure it was okay. All of a sudden, she started having pain and found out that she had a cancerous tumor in her liver the size of a tennis ball. We could not understand how it was not caught sooner. My mom called for a pastor and wanted to become a Christian. She changed so much. She remembered that she had prayed many years earlier for God to let her live long enough to see me graduate from the university. He answered that prayer. Before my mom passed away in 1994, she revealed to me that I had four half siblings in Singapore.

I decided to search for my family. I got an address in Singapore, where I was supposed to be able to find someone who knew my father. I met an old man that knew him, and with his help, I was able to locate my half siblings. It was a joyful time for me. I noticed that I was much more like this part of my family than I was like my mom and her relatives. They were very nice and kind people. I was not a Christian at that time, but most of them were. In fact, I found out that my father had become a Christian before he died.

In 1995, I returned to Hong Kong to live with my stepfather. I felt the need to take care of him as repayment for his kindness to my mother during her illness. I got a job in the insurance business. Like my mom, I was very superstitious about things in life. I worried all the time. I reunited with my celebrity friends from my modeling days, and we often partied and smoked marijuana.

At 27 years old, I had a passion to do public speaking and did some radio hosting, but you had to have some claim to fame to get into that industry. That is when I decided to participate in the Miss Asia pageant. I did not win, but it was an interesting experience.

I continued to work in the insurance business, but in 1997, I suffered some big financial losses. In order to make it through, I had to borrow money. The interest rates were very high, and I was soon $150,000 in debt. I was having a hard time making the payments. I turned to idols and New Age practices, hoping they would bring me good luck and financial success, but I realized they brought me no peace or truth.

In 1998, I decided to go to Evangelical Community Church because I had a friend who attended that church. Soon, I decided to become a Christian, but I was still a little confused about Jesus being the one true God. I read the words of Jesus in John 14:6, *"Jesus said to him, 'I am the way, the truth, and the life. No one comes to the Father except through Me.'"* (ESV) I believed His words and decided to remove all of the idols from my home and life. I no longer associated with my friends who partied all the time. At church, I met new friends who met my needs. I prayed for the Lord to rescue me from my crushing debts. I still smoked marijuana occasionally, but I became convicted that it was wrong and I quit.

Because of the way I grew up, I still hate to see anyone be verbally abused by others. Because I never felt like anyone cared for me, I have become a deeply caring person. After five years of learning to control my finances, I became a top agent in my company and paid off all my debts. Because of my church, I learned more and more English. I believe that was God preparing me for my future husband.

In 2004, I was diligently praying for God to give me a good husband. By 2006, I was frustrated with waiting on the Lord to lead me to the right man. As I read God's word, He showed me Habakkuk 2:1-3, *"I will stand my watch and set myself on the rampart, and watch to see what He will say to me, and what I will answer when I am corrected. Then the LORD answered me and said: 'Write the vision and make it plain on tablets, that he may run who reads it. For the vision is yet for an appointed time; but at the end it will speak, and it will not lie. Though it tarries, wait for it; because it will surely come, it will not tarry.'"* (NKJ) I wrote down all the characteristics I hoped to find in the man God had chosen for me. I prayed that he would be taller than me, athletic, and God-fearing.

In December 2006, I met a man through an online matchmaking service. As we got to know one another, He agreed that my list described him well, except he did not really understand the God-fearing part. He was Swedish, and was the product of the traditional European church. He was "confirmed" as a child, but he did not have any relationship with Christ. He was willing to go to church and Bible study with me, though. His curiosity was piqued, and he even listened to biblical teaching on the internet. Before long, he became a Christian and was baptized. He developed a great heart for God and sought to follow His ways. We even kept ourselves pure until marriage. I am blessed to see how God has transformed my husband. At first, my pastor was concerned about us wanting to get married so quickly, but he soon realized that Marcus had a godly heart.

Strangely enough, I had found a wedding gown that fit me perfectly two months before I even met my husband-to-be. I bought it because it was simple and appropriate for the outdoor wedding I had always wanted. When we met and decided to get married, he wanted a church wedding, but it just would not work out that way. We ended up with a beautiful garden wedding on September 1, 2007. It started out as a rainy day, but I had peace in my heart that it would turn around. By the time of the wedding, it turned into a clear, hot day. God is good.

I know that our marriage would never work without Christ. We are from such different cultures. We like different foods, sports, and hobbies. It is only because of our relationship with the Lord that two people with such differences have come together in unity. We decided to wait a while to have a baby, but when we decided it was time, we could not get pregnant. We even tried in vitro fertilization, but we still did not conceive a child. God's will is always perfect, so we are content with our relationship, even without a child of our own.

Sometimes insurance agents have a hard time making friends, because everyone thinks you will try to sell them insurance all the time. I make friends very easily though. My clients and coworkers love me and become my friends, too. I guess it is because they can tell that I sincerely care about them. I often minister to them and have even led some to Christ. I had a very tough boss, who often made things difficult for me, but it drove me to work harder and become successful. That tough boss has now become a Christian, too.

God has definitely raised my life from the ashes. He has chosen me to demonstrate His grace and power. He has given me an opportunity to be a godly influence in the lives of many people. My husband does prison ministry in Hong Kong and other countries. We have even gotten to see his parents get baptized. I get along with my in-laws beautifully, even though there is a language barrier. I visit my half siblings in Singapore yearly. Three of them have renewed their relationship with the Lord.

Even though I do not have any parents on this Earth, my co-workers are like a real family. At work, my assistant, Jones, is like a loving daughter to me. At home, my helper, Bella, is like a mommy to my husband and me. Both of these friends are true helpers and prayer warriors in my life. My husband and I say a blessing prayer over each other every morning. God is using those prayers to bless us very much. I just want to say a special word of thanks to Marcus, Jones, and Bella as I close. This is my story of beauty from ashes, and I hope it will be a blessing to you.

## AUTHOR BIOGRAPHY

**Background**: Rebecca Kalioniemi was born and is a current resident of Hong Kong. She works as an Associate Director Wealth Management & Protection of AIA. She holds a B.A. in economics. In 2009, she was 1st runner up in the Mrs. World Hong Kong competition and was awarded the title of Mrs. Macau in 2009 and 2011 receiving the most whimsical costume award at the 2009 Mrs. World competition.

Within her profession, she has received 16 times MDRT where 4 times were COT (top 1% in the world insurance industry).

**Community/ Volunteer Services**: 10 Years of The ambassador of The CEO Foundation-foster program in Luyang, China for handicapped orphans (www.theceofoundation.org)

**Philosophy of Life or Favorite Quote/ Scripture:** For I know the plans I have for you," declares the Lord, "plans to prosper you and not to harm you, plans to give you hope and a future. Then you will call on me and come and pray to me, and I will listen to you. You will seek me and find me when you seek me with all your heart. I will be found by you," declares the Lord, "and will bring you back from captivity. I will gather you from all the nations and places where I have banished you," declares the Lord, "and will bring you back to the place from which I carried you into exile." (Jeremiah 29:11-14 NIV)

# TESTIMONY 4

## By Nieika Parks

I know that God has afforded me additional time on Earth to share how He gave me beauty for ashes. Today I share my story as a proud mother of a six-year-old boy, wife to my college sweetheart, and member of Delta Sigma Theta Sorority, Incorporated. I am an employee of FedEx Employee Benefits, using my PhD in Health Promotion to educate our diverse employee population. However, my "Beauty for Ashes" story began three years ago when I was the Director of Memphis City Schools' Office of Coordinated School Health.

At the time, I was responsible for overseeing the health crisis that our District was facing during the H1N1 flu virus pandemic. We had three children to experience untimely deaths from complications related to H1N1. This scare jolted our community, garnering local and national media coverage (http://www.wreg.com/wreg-swinefluhotline-story,0,3852942.story/   http://www.wmctv.com/global/story.asp?s=11213238).

It was a Monday evening, and I was poised to give a presentation to the Board of Education, and the general public, on H1N1 prevention measures. I had not been feeling well for weeks, but considering the demands of both my professional and personal life, I did not feel that I had time to seek care. This meeting was particularly important, as it was my opportunity to decrease the panic our community was feeling. Upon arrival, it was apparent that this meeting would be lengthy, but I could no longer hide my discomfort.

Immediately, following the meeting, I went to a Minor Medical Facility where I was told that I had a kidney infection. I was given a prescription for antibiotics with instructions to go home and rest. At home, I grew progressively worse. Being in tune with my body, I knew that I was experiencing a major health problem and needed to get to a hospital. At the hospital, I was examined and admitted. Within my week's stay, I collapsed from heart failure. My mother, a nurse practitioner, called code and the paddles were used to restart my heart. At 32 years of age, I was on life support for five days.

When I awakened, it was to everyone's amazement that I had no brain damage or other physical signs of my near death experience. I am fortunate to be among the five percent of people that have survived sudden cardiac arrest. Today, my heart and other major organs have completely recovered. I feel compelled to share my story, in the hope of informing others about the goodness of God. I want everyone to know that He still performs miracles.

Put yourself in my shoes. After being told about all that happened, my spirit was flooded with questions and confusion. I thought to myself, "How could I get sick?" I was the picture of health. I did not drink, smoke, or use drugs. I had served God since I came to Christ at the age of nine. I served as the health champion in my family, and in my occupation. Why would God allow this to happen to me?

I can testify wholeheartedly that God used my health scare to teach me several lessons and bring about spiritual growth in some areas. First, He required that I exercise my faith in Him. I have always been an outspoken Christian who encouraged others to live for Him. Now, it was time for my faith to be tested. Did I truly believe the scriptures in their entirety? As I sat in a hospital bed, unable to care for my child or even myself, I knew God had allowed this circumstance for my good. Romans 8:28 says, *"And we know that all things work together for good to them that love God, to them who are called according to his purpose."* (KJV) I was given an opportunity to live out what I talked about, and I knew that others were watching. I refused to be a hypocrite. I chose to use this opportunity to demonstrate devotion to God during difficulty.

Next, I learned to let God be the author of my story. We all know that ultimately He is in control, however, those of us who are overachievers like to have things planned out in an orderly fashion. What happens when things occur for which we have not planned? For the Christians, those times could be called God-ordained detours. I would have never chosen for this to happen to me, but God did, and He knows best. So how did I adjust and conform? I grew by accepting God's will for my life. Through acceptance, I began to embrace the fact that I am a heart disease survivor.

Afterward, God provided me with numerous platforms to share my story. For example, I currently serve as a spokesperson for the American Heart Association - MidSouth Affiliate, and chairperson for their Multi-Cultural Diversity Committee. This group supports causes like Go Red for Women and the local Heart Walk within our community. God added a new dimension to my educational credentials. He added a real-life health story to which others could relate to and from which they could learn.

Furthermore, my near death experience strengthened my resolve to be appreciative for all the blessings God has granted in my life. In 1 Thessalonians 5:18, the Bible says, "*In everything give thanks: for this is the will of God in Christ Jesus concerning you.*" (King James 2000 Bible) I have learned the importance of living each day to the fullest. "*Whereas ye know not what shall be on the morrow. For what is your life? It is even a vapour, that appeareth for a little time, and then vanisheth away*" (James 4:14 KJV).

I cherish my son and my husband more than ever. On the one year anniversary of my cardiac arrest, my mother came to town so we could deliver edible arrangements to the nursing staff that cared for me during my three week hospital stay. To let him know how phenomenal his staff is, I personally wrote a letter to the CEO of the hospital. I also wrote notes to each person that came by the hospital, sent a card in the mail, or called to pray with me over the phone during my time of difficulty. I wanted everyone to know that, collectively, my family and friends showered me with God's love when I needed it most.

## AUTHOR BIOGRAPHY

 Dr. Nieika Parks is a long-time resident of the Midsouth region, having received her background training from the University of Memphis where she earned a B.A. in Psychology and a Masters in Health Administration. In 2005, she completed her dissertation, the final component for her Ph.D. in Health Promotion and Health Education while enrolled at the University of Alabama at Birmingham and employed at the University of Tennessee Health Science Center (UTHSC).

She currently works at FedEx Express within Employee Benefits where she is responsible for communicating and training employees and management for successful implementation of the health/benefits plan designs and evaluating the annual benefits enrollment information to ensure effective usage of financial and employee resources. She establishes new processes to enhance employee's benefit experience through technology, resource tools, employee communications, education, and consumer engagement. She also provides onsite meetings and webinars to help employees understand the tools, resources, and programs available to them through existing and upcoming benefits packages.

In her former work within Memphis City Schools (MCS), she served as Director for Coordinated School Health (CSH) and was responsible for the administration, supervision, organization, and implementation of the health, physical education, and lifetime wellness curricula. She also supervised student health screenings, staff health fairs, and similar projects including grant-funded initiatives. She provided direction to school-based Healthy School Teams and the district-level School Health Advisory Council and staff development for CSH, Body Mass Index and Blood Pressure Screenings, the School Health Index, and the Healthy School Team Data Form. She launched four new school-based health clinics in Spring 2009.

With over seven years of experience in teaching and curriculum development, Dr. Parks has also had the privilege to provide education to medical students, college students, and the general public through her work with UTHSC, the University of Alabama at Birmingham (Schools of Education and Medicine), and the University of Memphis. She currently holds an adjunct professor position in the University of Memphis' Division of Health Administration. Current research interests include health technologies to improve opportunities for educating isolated clinicians and addressing health disparities among medically underserved populations, and strategies to leverage community-outreach programs into regional networks for expanded service, resource sharing, and policy guidance. Her passion is adolescent and child health.

Dr. Parks has had numerous opportunities to develop her leadership and coordination skills as a member of Epsilon Kappa Chapter of Delta Sigma Theta, Inc., American College of Health Care Executives, National Association of Health Services Executives and the Golden Key National Honor Society. She has also been privileged to speak at Yale University on the topic of "The Struggle of Black Students on Predominately White Campuses: The Black Graduate Perspective." Her most recent publication is within The Journal of Negro Education, Volume 78, Number 3 (Summer 2009). She co-authored "Before the Bell Rings: Implementing Coordinated School Health Models to Influence the Academic Achievement of African American Males" with Leon D. Caldwell, Abigail A. Sewell, and Ivory A. Toldson. She is a graduate of Leadership Memphis's Fasttrack, a program designed for young professional community leaders, and has participated in Meta-Leadership Training at Harvard University. She serves on the advisory boards of several local organizations including YMCA of Memphis and the MidSouth, American Heart Association, and Healthy Memphis Common Table.

# By Jonique Burton

In January 2009, my husband and I were expecting a baby. We were elated, and excitement was an understatement. Since I had two previous miscarriages, my doctor recommended that I undergo many tests to see if my child would have a disability. One of the tests was an amniocentesis. The results from this test determined that my baby would be born with Down Syndrome.

I can remember the phone call as if it was yesterday. I could not swallow, breathe, or think clearly. I didn't know who to call or what to do. I was numb from being in a state of shock. Who could have ever imagined a young, thriving couple would receive this news about their first-born?

My husband and I blamed each other, God, and our ancestry. We tried hard to figure out from whose genes this could have come. At first, we believed we were destined for failure. I worried about the situation instead of praying about the situation. I focused my energy on the problem instead of talking to God about the problem.

Once I was able to wrap my head around the situation, I began to seek God for answers. God impressed upon my heart that everything would be all right. He promised me that He would never leave me nor forsake me. He also reminded me that my baby girl was made in His image. After this conversation with God, I began to trust Him more. I put all of my burdens on His shoulders, and I knew I was safe.

In August 2009, Jillian Olivia was born. She was exactly what God told me. She was made in His image...PERFECT. I am so happy that we did not listen to those who had advised us to abort Jillian. My baby girl was born without sickness. This is rare for children diagnosed with Down Syndrome, but God is a healer, provider and protector, just to name a few aspects of who He is.

All of her tests came back negative; no leukemia, no thyroid issues, no kidney issues, no vision problems. She is the apple of our eyes. She has a few developmental delays, but is progressing like a typical three year old in many ways. I am proud to call her my daughter and would not trade her for anything in the world.

## AUTHOR BIOGRAPHY

Jonique Burton is a wife, mother, daughter, sister, and friend. She is a woman of God who believes in trusting God in every situation in her life. Jonique was born in the sultry, southern city of New Orleans, Louisiana. After completing high school, she went on to attend Tennessee State University in Nashville, Tennessee. While at Tennessee State University, Jonique completed a Bachelor of Science – Mathematics degree.

Jonique's passion has always been to help others, but especially in the subject area of mathematics. When a lucrative career opportunity became available in Houston, Texas, Jonique accepted the challenge to become a secondary mathematics teacher in the public school setting. Jonique continued her education at Texas Southern University. She received a Masters of Public Administration and a Principals Mid-Management certification.

Upon completion of those academic achievements, Jonique began to date a wonderful man, James Burton. After two years of courting, Jonique and James decided to demonstrate their mutual faith and love, as they became one in marriage. Later, Jonique moved to Indianapolis, Indiana with her husband. Upon moving to Indianapolis, Jonique decided to further her education, and received her Education Specialist – School Superintendency (EdS) from Ball State University.

Currently, Jonique lives in Indianapolis with her husband, James, and daughter, Jillian. She works as a Student Programs Advisor/Crisis

Administrator at a prestigious public high school. While juggling life, Jonique is completing her Doctorate of Educational Administration (EdD) from Ball State University. Jonique is an active member in her sorority, which is committed to community service. Jonique is also an active member of her local church in Indianapolis – New Life Worship Center. As a wife, mother, secondary educator, student, and committed community and public servant, her life never has a dull moment.

GET TO KNOW: *Jillian*

Down Syndrome Indiana

## TESTIMONY 6

# By Jurrita Williams

The power of knowing His love finally arrested me.

I was 20 years old, just doing my thing while home from college. One day, as I was visiting my grandmother, I wondered aloud, "Grandma, have you read the WHOLE Bible?" With a resounding, "Yes, several times", it made me feel a little sick. I had accepted Jesus off a "mourners bench" back in the 80's and had never read the Book about the One who got me off that bench. Although I had never missed a Sunday at church growing up, (okay, maybe once or twice), that day was the beginning of a journey that introduced me to beauty instead of ashes.

I would not really say I was a *bad* child, but as I said before, I did my thing. When I did something wrong, there was always that really bad feeling that God was going to get me. As a young girl, I would sing, "Jesus loves me this I know, for the Bible tells me so", but I never really *felt* His love. I never really *knew* that love about which I was singing.

You need to understand how I viewed God. I had always seen Him as a mean, angry God who was ready to punish everybody. Even though my parents made sure my siblings and I were in church Sunday after Sunday, the knowledge that the almighty God really loved me deeply and intimately never made the trip from my head to my heart. The difference came when I started to read His love letter to the world (the Bible). I came to understand that it was not just to the world in general, but a personal message to *me* as well. Once I had that conversation with my grandmother, it started me on what would become a never-ending love journey with the One who *is* Love.

I decided to start at the beginning of the Bible, reading one chapter a night, no matter what. At that point, I was not on a journey to find that for which my heart had been longing. I wanted to read the whole Bible, just to say I had read it. I was not setting out to *live right*; I actually just wanted to read the Bible because I was amazingly ashamed that I had never read it on my own. However, once I uncovered for myself His intense love for *me*, it was absolutely impossible to remain the same.

I think every woman wants to be loved. I believe every woman wants to be chosen, and I am that woman. God had given me so much in my life. I grew up in a wonderful family. I got to be homecoming queen, be a cheerleader, wear the latest fashions, etc., but I still felt unloved. I just never felt that I was good enough. My soul was dry, and my heart was thirsty. Jesus said to another thirsty woman, in John 4:14 (NIV), "*But whoever drinks the water I give them will never thirst*", and as we used to say, "He ain't never lied."

I have not had to drink from the well of loneliness, self-centeredness, or feelings of being unloved again. That does not mean the thoughts do not come, but in His Word I gain the daily strength to know that I do not have to drink at those wells anymore. I have to be intentional about receiving His unfailing and *unworked for* love, but He gives me His beauty for my ashes everyday through His Son, Jesus Christ.

It gives me life to tell about His unfailing love, because it radically changed my life, and I pray it does yours, too. It gave me purpose when I found out He not only loved me, but He *wanted* me. There is nothing like knowing you are chosen, accepted, approved and loved...*deeply loved*. That kind of unwavering love and affection can only come from above. I do not mean the second floor of Dillard's, Macy's or Neiman Marcus, but from above and beyond anything this world or anyone in it could ever offer. The Message in Ephesians 1:4 (NIV) says, "*Long before he laid down earth's foundations, he had us in mind, had settled on us as the focus of his love, to be made whole and holy by his love.*" It is not about our love for Him, or what we have to do to please Him, but *all* about His love for you and me.

Let *His love* heal you and make you whole today. It did those things for me, and it keeps on healing me every day. No matter who you are, where you are, what you have done, or how long you have been doing it, please allow His perfect love to arrest you, and then set you free. Allow Him to take your hand and your heart, and walk you through *your ashes* into *His beauty.*

Thanks for the opportunity to share how His life is changing my life.

## AUTHOR BIOGRAPHY

Jurrita is a native of Tuscaloosa, AL and the 2nd daughter of Pastor James and Doris Williams. She received a wonderful heritage of loving Christ from them both.

Having spent 5 years in the field of education in Montgomery, AL, God's destiny drew her into full time ministry. Jurrita has served as Youth minister at First Baptist Church in Newbern, AL where her father serves as Pastor and ministers at various churches and conferences.

Presently, Jurrita serves as Youth Pastor at Hightown Church of God in Northport, AL where Marvin D. Cherry serves as Senior Pastor. At Hightown, she leads a Youth Ministry called XCeL (Exalting Christ's Everlasting Love).

Above all else, Jurrita realizes the overwhelming and unfailing love God has for her through His Son Jesus. She lives to make HIS name famous and desires to spend the rest of her days letting the world know of His love.

# TESTIMONY 7

## By Juanita Ingram, Esq.

I can remember it like it was yesterday. I was sitting in my car in the parking lot outside of the doctor's office. I just left from a follow-up appointment with one of the doctors from the team of gastroenterologist specialists that followed me throughout my first pregnancy. I sat in the car crying because I had just been told that I should come to grips with the fact that I should give up on having a second child.

My daughter was just ten weeks old, and we had been through an ordeal getting her here! Sitting in the car, I began to weep as the words spoken by my OBGYN four weeks prior, and now my GI specialist, began to sink in. They both advised and admonished me from ever getting pregnant again and attempting to have a second child. I always dreamed of how my pregnancy experience would unfold. I knew that I wanted two children - a boy and a girl. My grandmother even gave me a portrait many years ago depicting an angel watching over a little boy and a little girl. I had it displayed in my home for years before I even started to try and conceive children. But now sitting in the car on that hot day in June, I began to mourn the death of a portion of that dream.

I didn't know at the time my husband and I conceived our daughter that I would be in for such an uphill battle. Weeks into my pregnancy, I began to feel extremely ill. I certain symptoms that I passed off as normal first trimester illnesses that most women experience. But that all changed as I began to get more and more ill. I had a tremendous amount of pain emanating from lower digestive tract. Every time I would eat I would be in so much pain that I couldn't breathe. I could barely eat and

34

my doctors discovered that a portion of my lower digestive tract seemed to be in complete and total paralysis. They had never observed such an occurrence in a pregnant woman before. Fast-forward a few months – two OBGYNs, three GI specialists, two midwives, and one alternative medicine naturalist later – I was finally diagnosed with ulcerative colitis.

I was told that I would probably not carry my child full term and that I would likely lose her before making it to month five. I was also told that I was at a high risk of having my lower digestive tract (that's my nice way of saying my colon) perforated or ruptured which would cause internal bleeding, infection, and possible death. I wasn't gaining weight – and neither was my child. There was a blockage in my lower digestive region that they couldn't explain or discover the root cause. They could see it on the ultrasound. I was pregnant and I couldn't take the traditional medication that they would prescribe under normal circumstances. I didn't know it at the time, but my inability to take the traditionally prescribe medications would later prove to be a blessing in disguise because a few of the traditional medications cause serious side effects that can cause difficulties in fertility for women. But at the time, it didn't feel like a blessing at all.

During my pregnancy I also developed a heart murmur and had constant extreme fatigue, malnutrition, black out and/or fainting spells, and an extreme amount of pain. For the entire nine months of my pregnancy, I suffered.

I also began to emotionally feel discouraged. I felt like a failure as a mother already and I hadn't even delivered her yet. I could barely keep anything down and when I did eat, I would experience an excruciating amount of pain from the ulcers which developed. Also, because a portion of my lower intestines was now in a state of paralysis and inflamed, the nurturance from my food intake wasn't being absorbed into my body properly. They child that I had prayed for wasn't growing at the proper rate. I was a mess. I worried; I prayed; and I cried out to God for Him to heal me and to take this affliction away.

But, for the entire nine months, I suffered. I had dreams of having a wonderful and peaceful pregnancy – but that wasn't my portion. I was concerned about the level of stress that I was under and what effect it would have on our child. I was also concerned about my future professionally. Here I was, a prominent lawyer working 50 to 60 hour weeks and at the upswing of my career. Yet now I was forced to go on bed rest and stop practicing for the last four months of my pregnancy. Only one person on my job understood what was happening to me.

I remember one of my legal colleagues came into my office, looked at me, and began to cry. She walked in as I was lying on the floor dictating a memo into my hand held recorder. I was lying on the floor because it was the only way I could breathe sometimes after lunch due to the level of the pain I would experience after eating food. She said, "What are you doing? How are you still coming in here everyday? I am worried about you. You don't look right. Why are you so small?" I was almost six months pregnant and I wasn't really showing. I had only gained five to six pounds. I didn't even tell anyone on my job that I was pregnant until my fifth month because my doctors didn't think I would be able to carry full term. I saw the fear and worry on her face and it scared me. There was nothing in the "*What to Expect While You're Expecting*" book that covered what I was experiencing. It took months before I could even get a proper diagnosis of what was happening to me.

While on bed rest during my last trimester, I remember feeling such waive of heaviness come over me. My daughter wasn't gaining enough weight. My team of doctors was concerned about her development. I had to eat more no matter how much pain I was in. I felt so isolated because no one seemed to fully get what I was going through, nor did anyone even seem to know what (UC)/colitis was. I didn't even know what it meant. My doctors had never observed such an occurrence in a pregnant female. It was as if my entire colon just stopped working. I didn't have a full understanding of what was happening medically, I just knew that I wanted it to stop. But it didn't stop.

I know what it is like to cry out in pray day after day for God to heal you – and to continue to wait. I felt like I was failing at everything – everything except for my faith. That was all I had. And it would prove to be enough. As it says in Romans 8:26 (ESV) "Likewise the Spirit helps us in our weakness. For we do not know what to pray for as we ought, but the Spirit himself intercedes for us with groanings too deep for words". I knew that God heard my cry and through my tears, He not only heard but understood what I needed.

Around 37 weeks, my doctors made the call that my body couldn't take much more. My labor was induced and I delivered a perfectly healthy baby girl who weighted a little over 5lbs. I remember feeling so relieved that she missed being labeled "low birth weight" by a few ounces – we fought every ounce! She was beautiful, healthy, and perfect. God had given me beauty for my suffering. She was everything I had prayed for and five years later, she is one of the brightest in her class! My symptoms seemed to subside and go into remission several months after my delivery and with the help of my alternative medicine naturalist, I was back to living a functional digestive life for the most part. I still had some symptoms and digestive pain on occasion but they were manageable.

Deep down inside I was heartbroken at the thought of only have one child but I was equally grateful to have her. I often praise God for my daughter. The one they told me wouldn't make it to be delivered. The child that they said was not developing properly and may not survive. I praised God with all that I had for that blessing and I became content with not being able to have a second child. She was a beautiful bundle of joy and she was enough.

With that background, you can imagine my reaction seventeen months after my daughter was born when we discovered that I was pregnant again!!! To this day my husband and I really don't know where #2 came from!!! Well, we kind of know – but seriously, we were trying everything possible to NOT get pregnant again. When my OBGYN and GI specialist said that we barely made it through the first pregnancy and that I should never seek to have more children, I took it to heart. So, when I found out I was pregnant again I collapsed to the floor and cried. See, I had given up on having that second child that I so very much longed for. I believed the doctors when they told me that it was too much on my body, that next time my intestines would most likely response the same way again and that I would probably not be successful in carrying a second child. They told me it was too great a health risk. Remember, I had prayed that I would have a daughter and a son but I listened to their report and I thought that dream was impossible now. So when I learned I was pregnant again, I cried. I was afraid that I might die or that this time around and I would lose the pregnancy.

While my second pregnancy was certainly not without its tests and trials, it was again a time which demonstrated the grace, mercy, and provision of the Lord. This time around, my alternative medicine specialist discovered a natural medicine which was a tremendous help with my lower intestinal problems. As predicted, with this pregnancy my UC/colitis came out of remission and flared up again. Everything function that the colon should do, it didn't. But with the help of a natural medicine, which had recently been approved for pregnant women to take, my experience this time around was much less painful. I was able to eat with very little pain and this time the ulcers in my lower intestinal tract only manifested toward the end of my pregnancy not the entire 9 months like before. I did experience some severe pre-term labor issues but that was completely manageable. And although I was on bed rest again for four months, it proved to be such a blessed and miraculous time. At the end of it all, I held in my arms a beautiful 7lb baby boy! He is the son I had given up on being able to have. The one the doctors said I wouldn't be able and shouldn't even attempt to have. I know exactly how Hannah felt when she said, "Oh, my lord! As your soul lives, my lord, I am the woman who stood here beside you, praying to the LORD. For this boy I prayed, and the LORD has given me my petition which I asked of Him. So I have also dedicated him to the LORD; as long as he lives he is dedicated to the LORD." 1 Samuel 1:26-28 (NIV). God had given me the secret desires of my heart. He gave me joy for my sorrow.

I rarely spoke about these issues prior to now. I didn't want to dwell on the time when I was weak, sick, and discouraged. But the proof of God's purpose in our lives can be seen through the scares. If we hide those scares, how will can others see them and be encouraged? So often in life it is our natural response to cover our weaknesses. But often the place of weakness that we want to hide is the place where God produces the strength that He wants to show the world. As it says in Corinthians 12:9-10 (ESV) "But He said to me, "My grace is sufficient for you, for my power is made perfect in weakness. Therefore I will boast all the more gladly of my weaknesses, so that the power of Christ may rest upon me. For the sake of Christ, then, I am content with weaknesses, insults, hardships, persecutions, and calamities. For when I am weak, then I am strong."

Through all of this, not only was I blessed to have the two beautiful children that I prayed for and desired – but God also qualified and enabled me to minister to those who are sick, in need of healing, and waiting on a miracle. I was also asked to be a spokesperson/champion for the UK Chrons & Colitis organization in order to help others be encouraged and informed about colitis. I am living proof that God can and will give you comfort for your mourning, joy for your sorrow, and beauty for your ashes.

Be blessed.

## AUTHOR BIOGRAPHY

***If you ask Juanita Ingram, Esq., she will tell you she is just an ordinary woman*** who has experienced some extraordinary blessings. Originally from the USA, Mrs. Ingram has made the United Kingdom her home where she represents the contemporary global woman with grace, humility & style!

A wife, mother of two, attorney, author, speaker, producer, entrepreneur, and international beauty queen; this woman of substance has been making an impact around the world. As Founder and President of the Happy To Be You Ministries Inc., Juanita often serves as keynote speaker on topics of self esteem, discovering self-worth and identity through the Word of God, and goal attainment. She is a frequent a volunteer for several international organizations such as Dress For Success Worldwide, which focuses on providing the necessary resources to increase self sufficiency and confidence in women and youth. She also serves as the Director of the Girls of Greatness UK, a program, which assists young women to develop healthy levels of self-esteem, embracing their unique qualities, accomplishing their dreams, and making a difference in this world. She also serves as the national cover girl and Champion for Moms for the Best for Babes charity in the US.

She most recently has been engaged on an international book tour with her books, *"Winning with Christ – Finding the Victory in Every Experience"* and **The Wonderfully Made Pals**™ series, a multi-cultural Christian children's book series, with current volumes that include *"Kind Kinsley"*, *"Confident Keynan"*, *"Generous Gregorio"*, and *"Wonderfully Made Wanita"*.

Mrs. Ingram is also the creator, co-director and executive producer of a new Christian docu-reality series – **Modern Day Esther** (www. moderndayesther.com), which highlights Christian woman giving a different (and Christ-centered) response to life's drama.

Mrs. Ingram graduated from Tennessee State University (*Cum* Laude) where she obtained her Bachelor's degree in accounting and subsequently received her Jurist Doctorate and MBA from the University of Memphis. She is a licensed attorney in two states in America and is currently obtaining a Masters of Law degree (LLM) from the University of London. Mrs. Ingram has obtained both large firm and in-house counsel experience having successfully practiced law for over 11 years.

She is the first African-American woman to win the titles of Mrs. Universe United Kingdom 2013, Mrs. Universe E-Vote 2013, Ms. World International 2012, Mrs. World Great Britain (UK) 2011, Mrs. US Beauties 2009, and Mrs. Indiana United States 2007.

If asked, Mrs. Ingram would say that faith and family are her top priority and always come first! She enjoys traveling around the world with her husband and children. Her favorite hobbies include reading, painting, music (piano & flute), and motivational speaking.

With the innate desire to give back and leave a lasting footprint, Juanita has often been called the "giving soul".

To find out more about Mrs. Ingram, please feel free to visit www. happy2bu.org or www.juanitaingram.com.

## By Neysa Taylor

## MY HUSBAND CHEATED ON ME,
## AND I AM A BETTER WIFE BECAUSE OF IT

Yes, you read the title right. My husband cheated on me, and I am a better wife because of it. It is true, but before sisters start rolling their eyes, let me first back up a bit. No one deserves to be cheated on. No one can make a person cheat or prevent a person from cheating. I can honestly say that dealing with the infidelity, and the long-term emotional scars from it, are things that I would not wish on my enemy.

It was hard, and it still is hard because this was not a one-time mistake that we could easily forget. No, my husband had an affair that resulted in the birth of twin boys. That situation alone is enough to send most people to divorce court. Initially, that was my reaction. I was quick to say, "Adios", but honestly, God kept bringing me back. Each time I looked at how messed up the situation was, I kept seeing cracks in my own armor. What does that mean? It means that my husband did the unthinkable and had to deal with the consequences, but the situation made me face my own demons as well.

What demons? I had to deal with my parents' divorce. I had to stop crucifying my father for his own missteps. I had to let that baggage go and define my marriage for myself, not as a carbon copy of theirs. I had to slay the judgmental demon. I was quick to say, "I would never..." and, "If that happened to me, I'd do..." I learned that you cannot judge someone's decisions or journey. While I was judging others, I had a fear of being judged. I had to put that fear down and learn to live as a flawed, but beautifully authentic person.

I had to slay my tongue. Actually, I am still fighting that one. I learned that the childhood saying, "Sticks and stones may break my bones, but words will never hurt me", is a lie. Words hurt. Words linger and have power. Words can eat away at the soul of your spouse. As a wife who wielded words like a sharpened sword, I learned the power of staying silent; of allowing my spouse to make a mistake without saying, "I told you so." I learned the power of speaking words of praise and love. I learned how important it is to lose an argument sometimes in order to gain harmony in the home.

I had to kill my idea of what my marriage could be or what my spouse could become. I mistakenly thought that pushing my marriage and mate to be their best was my job. Well, part of that is true, but not at the expense of appreciating where they are right now. I have to love my husband exactly as he is right now and encourage him forward, not nag him forward.

I had to battle my false idols. I had to quit worshiping material things, my kids, and my spouse. In my darkest hour, I had to seek God and rely on Him. I had to get to the point where I honestly *believed.* Once my faith in God was restored, and I was truly seeking Him, everything else fell into place.

I cannot lie and say it was easy. It wasn't, but at some point I had to turn my attention away from what he was doing and my hatred for the mistress, toward myself and my God. It was hard work. I had to open up my Bible and really take comfort in the words. I had to realize that the Bible was God's yearbook. There was nothing that I was facing that He had not already worked out in the lives of others, and the Bible documented it all.

I admit I was out of practice. I had to surround myself His words. I kept a list of go-to scriptures EVERYWHERE. I kept Jeremiah 29:11 (NIV), *"For I know the plans I have for you, declares the LORD, plans for welfare and not for evil, to give you a future and a hope"*, at my desk. Isaiah 41:10 (NIV), *"Fear not, for I am with you; be not dismayed, for I am your God; I will strengthen you, I will help you, I will uphold you with my righteous right hand"*, was on my work notebook. I kept scripture on my bathroom mirror. I had reminders in my cell phone to pause and pray. I wrapped myself in God.

I was broken, tired, and downtrodden. After making a decision to not only chase God, but also to say, "Yes", to whatever God told me to do, my life began to turn around. It did not magically make my husband come to his senses, but he was no longer my concern. God was my concern. Matthew 6:33-34 (NIV) says, *"But seek first his kingdom and his righteousness, and all these things will be given to you as well. Therefore, do not worry about tomorrow, for tomorrow will worry about itself. Each day has enough trouble of its own."* That is exactly what I did.

Now, I can say I am a better wife than I was six years ago. The reason I can say that is that I am a better *person* now than I was six years ago. I had to go through the proverbial valley to learn to deal with my demons. Someone once asked me, "Knowing what you know now, if you had to do it all over again, would you? The pain? The tears? All of it?" That question made me pause. While I would not rush to sign up for the agony, I would like to think I would go through it again if those six years of turmoil were minor speed bumps on an 80-year loving covenant. Actually, I would do it again, because I know that the painful lessons have made me really get to know myself, and more importantly, my Father. For Him, I would gladly repeat the class.

## AUTHOR BIOGRAPHY

*Grateful, blessed,* and *loved* are the words that describe me best. I am a "real-talk prayer warrior." I love God, and I am constantly amazed that He loves me so much. I take pride in being called a wife, and I love being a mother of four. I am an award-winning journalist in Nashville, Tennessee and the owner of Myriad Media, Inc., an event scripting boutique firm.

# TESTIMONY 9

## *By Joyce Penas Pilarsky*

As a little girl, I prayed for God to bless me, as well as those around me. To make a way for the creation of schools that would enable all of the children including myself, to build a better future. The people around me lacked faith, they centered their jokes on me; but my faith was as strong as a mustard seed. Even as a child my faith wouldn't waver, for I knew that God would provide, in His time, the needs that I diligently asked for.

I continually praise God, and give Him thanks. I am so grateful that both my parents brought me up to know about God. They continually taught me the Bible and how to pray. I was raised in an environment where talking to God was vital. Everything of importance was thoroughly discussed with the Lord. I grew up in the Manila, Philippines, a place where the need for proper education was intense. Starting at a very young age, my father began to instill in his children the importance of education in our lives. He longed for us to study well and dreamed that all of his children would finish our studies. My father shared with us on many occasions his own hardships and struggles growing up as an orphan, having been placed in an abusive environment, and expected to work instead of study.

Despite all the turmoil surrounding my father's childhood, he persevered. Utilizing his strong faith in God, he was able to overcome the obstacles life placed before him. Even walking to school with shoes so dilapidated that his feet touched the dirt, making them cracked and sore was not enough to deter him. As a young adult, father went to Manila, where he continued to study, as well as work, to finance his education. My father worked his way up to become Chief of the Navy, but continued to pursue his education with diligence, often studying late into the evenings. He finally achieved his goal of becoming a lawyer.

My father is the kind of man who truly lives his faith. After becoming a lawyer, he would defend clients who could only afford to pay him with a chicken, some eggs, or baskets of fruit. It was my father's heart-felt desire that even those who could not afford the fare to travel to and from his office have legal counsel, in those instances, my father would provide legal counsel pro-bono, as well as pay for their travel.

This was not an easy life for my family. My mother was a housewife, loving, strong and as generous as my father. My mother's convictions were as strong as my father's, and together they held a united front for God. They instilled this legacy into their children, reminding us, as well as all those around them, that God is good, that He is always with us, and that having faith makes us wise.

My father died unexpectedly when he was in his fifties. This left my mother, who was around forty at the time, with no job skills and seven children to care for at home. My father had made provisions for his family prior to his death, however, the man entrusted with my father's insurance premiums, stole the money and disappeared. This left our family in dire circumstances. By the grace of God, my mother was able to find work. She had to go to London, where she worked three jobs. This left the job of parenting five younger brothers and sisters to me. With God's help, I was able to manage, even finding a job as a model.

God began to open doors in my life. I was able to volunteer at our church on charity missions, distributing essentials, as well as teaching the Bible to the poor. God's grace began to abound in my life, I was a house model at the Stargazer Silahis hotel, as well as at the Hyatt Regency Manila. Then I was presented with an opportunity to become a flight attendant at the Saudi Airlines, despite the age limit. This increase in salary allowed me to help more people. Through the Grace of God, we were able to start the Gintong Paled Foundation. With the help of sister Dulia Furones, we were able to start schooling children.

Through the years, God has provided me with a route to achieve education for the children in the area. I met and married a man who is as dedicated to the cause as I am. Together, we founded the Jocelyn and Gunter Pilarsky Foundation in 2011. I'm still in awe of the work of God when I see the children flourish. It is amazing to see these once homeless children, who resorted to petty crimes in the streets, transformed to educated children with a real chance at a future.

The Bible tells us that if you ask it will be given to you, seek and you will find. Knock and the door will be opened to you. I am blessed to experience this daily. In the last year, we have finished a floating school for children of the Manobo tribe, as well as a floating library. Our work continues as we keep my father's dream alive. I pray that one day our work can build much needed hospitals, providing medicine to the poor. I know that whatever God desires for my life will happen in due season. I am so thankful for all that he has allowed to happen through me.

## AUTHOR BIOGRAPHY

Joyce Penas Pilarsky is a jewelry and fashion designer, fashion model, painter, singer, host, and author. She holds a Bachelor of Science in Education Major in English from St. Paul College Manila. She is a former flight attendant with Philippine Airlines and Saudi Arabian Airlines. She was awarded Most Outstanding Filipino Artist in Baden Wurttemberg, Germany 2007 and 2011. She also received the 2012 Modern Day Hero Award in Philippines. She is president of the FGC Filipino German club in Karlsruhe Germany and the International director Rotary Club in San Marcelino branch Philippines. She has held the titles of Mrs. Philippines Germany 2000 and Ms. Philippines MWI International 2013.

# TESTIMONY 10

## By Valerie Thomas

I am the seventh child out of a family of nine. I grew up in Prince Georges County, Maryland in a Baptist Pastors home. I was conceived in the back seat of a 1957 Chevy. However, this was not made known to me as a child. The first reference made to this realization came at a large prayer meeting I attended, when the preacher said to no one in particular, "you may have been conceived in the back of a 1957 Chevy". In fact, this revelation was made known to me, through the Spirit of God. I heard these words as though the Lord was speaking them from his own mouth into my ears. Without question, I knew those words were spoken to me.

The Lord was trying to reveal this to me, yet at this time, I was still apprehensive. I knew that I was the black sheep of the family, and this could be the key as to why. Was it possible, that my father held resentment over the fact that I was not his biological child? On Sunday's, it seemed that my father would preach an effective sermon to the congregation, then transform into a completely different person upon arriving home. This person he became was filled with anger and rage. An angry spirit can't reside within a holy temple. Many times he would succumb to the demon, expressing violence upon the members of his own household.

I was protected from this violence by divine intervention. Whenever my father raised his fist to strike me, it would become frozen in mid-air. It was as if he seen or heard an angel, or perhaps the voice of God, rallying for my defense. I know that if he had been allowed to strike me with such force, it would have meant certain death.

During my father's bouts of rage, he would say, "one day I will tell you something". I often wonder if it would have been better if he have told me early on, instead of always wondering why I was unworthy of his love. Many times, I was isolated from my family, left alone to fend for myself. On more than one occasion, my mother and I were threatened with a gun. This created a distance between my mother and me, as she withdrew more and more to save me from my father's wrath.

Over the years, I would sense this evil spirit. It would hold a haunting presence over my life, showing up in my bedroom, where it would strangle me. The presence would hold me to the point where I was totally paralyzed. My only hope laid in the relationship I had with my heavenly Father. When I called upon the name of "Jesus", immediately I was set free. This was not something I was taught, nor told to do, it was instinct. God had revealed a strategy of survival, to break the chains that bound me. I know that trusting in Jesus, saved my life on more than one occasion. Luke 10:19- *I have given you authority to trample on snakes and scorpions and to overcome all the power of the enemy; nothing will harm you.* (NIV)

I didn't get confirmation from one of my parents until right after the birth of my first child. My mother told me it wouldn't be a good idea to contact my father. She then proceeded to confirm what the voice of God had been trying to tell for the last few years.

I wasn't aware that the hatred of my father had over taken me. This was revealed to through the Spirit of God as well. I heard the words, "I'm going to give you love for your father." As in all things, God speaks truth, and the love for my father grew in my heart. During this process, I realized that I must find forgiveness for all that my father put our family through. I could hear the Lord speak to my soul, speaking this verse into my heart, Matthew 6:14-15-*For if you forgive men when they sin against you, your heavenly Father will also forgive you. But if you do not forgive men their sins, your Father will not forgive your sins.* (NIV)

God is so good, and by listening to His voice, I was able to overcome the obstacles that Satan placed before me. I forgave my father with a loving heart, and we were able to reconcile, forming a loving relationship before his death.

## AUTHOR BIOGRAPHY

 My name is Valerie Thomas. I was born and raised in Lanham, Maryland. I currently hold a degree in Administration, Criminal Justice, Masters in Education, and sabbatical on Doctorate in Strategic Leadership. I am CEO & Founder of Lighthouse Christian Retreat. I am a Minister at Action Chapel Virginia, where Bishop Kibby Otto is presiding Bishop. One of my favorite Scriptures is: I Chronicles 29:11-13

11 Thine, O LORD is the greatness, and the power, and the glory, and the victory, and the majesty: for all that is in the heaven and in the earth is thine; thine is the kingdom, O LORD, and thou art exalted as head above all.

12 Both riches and honour come of thee, and thou reignest over all; and in thine hand is power and might; and in thine hand it is to make great, and to give strength unto all.

13 Now therefore, our God, we thank thee, and praise thy glorious name.

My prayer for you is that you may know the power in forgiveness and walking in love.

I'm so grateful to Juanita Ingram for giving me the honor of participating in this endeavor to touch many lives for God our Heavenly Father.

# TESTIMONY 11

## *By Anonymous*

At the age of 24, I found myself not only dating, but engaged to an emotionally, verbally, and physically abusive person. I often look back and wonder how on earth I got to that place.

Let me start out by saying that NO woman is purposed and placed on this earth to be abused in any manner – verbally, emotionally, or physically. Psalm 11:5 states, "The LORD tests the righteous, but his soul hates the wicked and the one who loves violence" (ESV). *God has not placed anyone here on earth to be abused at the hands of another.* If you or someone you know is in this type of relationship, seek help and safety immediately.

When I look back on my situation, I have to take responsibility for choosing to be with a person like that. Not only did I initially choose him, but I chose to stay. When I first met him, I knew I should have turned the other way and kept walking. He was a Muslim, and I was a Christian. The Bible is clear that as Christians, we are not to be yoked with unbelievers (2 Corinthians 6:14). While this verse is not specifically speaking to marriage or dating and speaks to a broader association, it certainly is applicable to whom we choose to date.

I knew we were not evenly yoked, but my walk with the Lord was rather lukewarm at the time. My self-esteem was low because I also didn't fully understand who I was in Christ; that I was royalty. I made poor decisions and choices when it came to men during that time in my life. It is impossible to make wise decisions when you don't take the time to fortify and grow in your relationship with the Lord. In addition, obedience to God's word is for your own good. I was fornicating at the time, so there was no way I could have the spiritual clarity to decide what was best for me in the arena of dating. God calls us to be abstinent until marriage for a reason. Sin places distance between you and the Lord - plain and simple. I am a living witness that, as women, we lose the ability to think clearly and evaluate a man's relationship with Christ until we (1) take the time to evaluate and nurture our own walk with the Lord, and (2) abstain from fornication so that we have closeness with the Lord and discernment that comes from Him.

I lacked the ability to discern this person's abusive, controlling, and manipulating spirit from the outset because I was young, naïve, and uncommitted to following God's commandments fully. God's rules and commandments are there for our protection. If we abide by them, they prevent us from finding ourselves in some hurtful and dangerous situations. Please understand, I am not suggesting that I am responsible for his actions. It was not my fault that he chose to be abusive, but we must all evaluate the choices that we made when we find ourselves in situations like these. We should ask what we could have done differently. We must learn from them in order for history not to repeat itself. The choices we make have serious outcomes, and I had to face the fact that I chose to be with him knowing that he had abusive tendencies. I also chose to stay as long as I did.

I would also like to speak to anyone who is a friend or a family member of someone who is in this type of situation. You must never give up praying and voicing your love and support for them. You must let them know of your disapproval of the abuse, and then offer to help them. One of the most hurtful parts of this experience was how my own family never really stepped up to the plate and confronted this guy the way they should have. I can recall crying as I read Genesis 42:21, *"And they said one to another, 'We are verily guilty concerning our brother, in that we saw the anguish of his soul, when he besought us, and we would not hear; therefore is this distress come upon us'" (KJV)*. Sure, my father may have said something to him in a somewhat direct yet polite way, but had it been my daughter, no abuser would have been welcome in my home – not ever. I would have helped her pack her things when she expressed how badly she wanted to leave. Most of my immediate family members knew of his controlling and emotionally abusive ways. They all knew how he had shaken me and thrown me over a table. They knew how he would verbally abuse me just before we visited them, and how I always looked as though I had been crying. People like to believe that verbal abuse is okay, but love doesn't hurt. Verbal abuse is still abuse, and it certainly displeases the Lord. As it says in Proverbs 10:11, "*The mouth of a righteous man is a well of life: but violence covereth the mouth of the wicked*" *(KJV)*.

They also knew how he spent thousands of dollars on me and supported me financially while in school. This lessened the burden for them. I remember calling home once and asking for money for study-aids. One of my family members told me to go ask him for it. That person knew what he was doing to me, but instead of providing a way for me to reduce my dependency upon him, and supporting me as they promised, they pushed me closer to him. He would buy me expensive things, and I was wearing a $15,000 engagement ring. To some, that was so impressive that they looked the other way concerning his abuse.

To the women who are currently in a situation like this, there will come a time when you have to be brave enough and resourceful enough to leave a financially co-dependent and abusive relationship. Trust in the Lord that He will provide for every need (Philippians 4:19). Make a plan of action to save up enough to leave. Believe what is set forth in *Psalm 9:9 and know that "The LORD also will be a refuge for the oppressed, a refuge in times of trouble" (KJV)*.

Ladies (and sometimes gentlemen), you are never responsible for what someone else chooses to do. Your abuser's actions toward you are not your fault, but you must make wise decisions from the outset so that you never choose to be with someone of this nature. I understand that there are times when a man will lie and pretend to be something that he is not. Sometimes people are not always who they present themselves to be. The person I was in a relationship with went so far as to lie and say he became a Christian to keep me.

With obedience and abstinence comes the level of clarity that you need as a single Christian to hear from God clearly, and discern who should and should not be in your life. When the Bible states that the wages of sin is death, it is so true. God's rules are there to protect us, not harm us. Dating someone who is not a believer, or even a lukewarm Christian who does not have a genuine desire to please the Lord, is a formula for heartache. Everyone has areas in their lives where they are works-in-progress, and I am not talking about a person who has a lot of *religion*. I am talking about whether or not that person has a real RELATIONSHIP with Christ. You cannot effectively and thoroughly evaluate the walk and character of someone else until you take sufficient time to evaluate and nurture your own walk with Christ.

Remember that you are a princess - the daughter of a King. You are royalty. You were never purposed to be hurt. Your Father in heaven has His best reserved for you. "Know ye not that ye are the temple of God, and [that] the Spirit of God dwelleth in you? If any man defile the temple of God, him shall God destroy; for the temple of God is holy, which [temple] ye are" (1 Corinthians 3:16-17 (NIV)). You are valuable in God's eyes; your whole self is regarded by God as a temple, a sacred place. Just as God does not want a temple defiled by violence, neither does God want you to be harmed. God's spirit dwells in you and makes you holy. You deserve to live without fear and without abuse.

If you have been or are currently in an abusive relationship, be certain that you leave, find shelter in a safe place, and get counseling. I pray that these scriptures aid in your healing as they have in mine. God bless.

Psalm 147:3 (NIV)
He heals the brokenhearted and binds up their wounds.

Isaiah 40:29-31 (NIV)
He gives power to the weak, and to those who have no might He increases strength...Those who wait on the LORD shall renew their strength; they shall mount up with wings like eagles, they shall run and not be weary, they shall walk and not faint.
Isaiah 54:14, 15 (NIV)

In righteousness you shall be established; you shall be far from oppression, for you shall not fear; and from terror, for it shall not come near you. Indeed they shall surely assemble, but not because of Me. Whoever assembles against you shall fall for your sake.

Isaiah 61:3 (NIV)

...To give them beauty for ashes, the oil of joy for mourning, the garment of praise for the spirit of heaviness...

# Testimony 12

## By ShaQuita C. Gatewood

### Pressing Toward my Destiny

Whenever I think about the earlier years of my life, I am overwhelmed with feelings of gratefulness. As the daughter of a teenage mother and a physically and mentally abusive father, I often struggled with why I was born into what seemed like such a dysfunctional family. I can remember daydreaming about what it would be like to have two parents who loved one another and lived in the same home. I dreamed about having my own room with my own bed. Based on the statistics that bombarded our community, I was destined for failure from the beginning simply because of the circumstances in which I was born.

As a child, I remember sitting in the corner of my aunt's home crying and asking God to protect my mother from my father. For the first eight years of my life, I vividly remember the yelling, screaming and physical abuse. As a joyful little girl who was full of dreams and ambitions, my heart was also always full of fear and worry. There were very few times in my life when I actually felt safe. Even when at church, I worried that my father would be outside the church once service was over. The only time I felt safe was when he was in jail. In my mind, I knew that he could not hurt my mother while he was in jail.

All I wanted as a child was a "normal" life - a life free from fear and worry. I can remember thinking that something must be wrong with me because my parents were not married, and they did not live in the same home. It was difficult to hear the children at my school talk about their moms and dads when I knew my situation was very different. As a child, I was forced to deal with adult issues at a very early age. I felt like I had to protect my mother. I had to stand up for her, even though I do not recall ever saying a word. It was something about my presence that made me believe he would not hurt her too badly if I were there. I am so thankful to my extended family, which included my grandparents and aunts. They did everything within their power to help me have a "normal" childhood. Unfortunately, I knew all too well how to put on the "everything-is-okay face", when, on the inside, I was crying out for help.

Even though I struggled with insecurities throughout elementary, middle, and high school, there was a still, quiet voice on the inside of me that pushed me to keep moving. I did not realize it then, but it was God's voice guiding me through the storm. I gave my life to the Lord when I was seven years old. I know it was only because of God, and the prayers of family members, that I was able to make it through those challenging times. I knew in my heart that my pain was temporary. His voice kept telling me to push beyond my pain. At that time of my life, I didn't know to read the Bible or to search out His Word for answers to my problems. I was simply guided by His voice and His ability to work through others around me. It is amazing how God thrust people into my life to serve as bridge builders. They pushed me into my destiny. If it was not for my family, some of my teachers, and certain people from my community, there is no way I would have made it through those valleys in my life.

Now that I am older, I realize just how much God's plan was being fulfilled in my life. No, I did not grow up in a perfect home, but I realized that my parents did the best they could at that time in their lives. I am thankful to say that I have a wonderful relationship with my mother and father. In spite of the statistics that told me I could not make it, God had a greater plan for my life. Not only did He allow me to graduate high school, but I also have a Bachelor's degree in Elementary Education, a Master's degree in Educational Leadership. Now, I am in the last year of my Doctoral program. He has blessed me with a wonderful loving husband who loves the Lord and our two children. Every dream I ever had as a little girl, God has brought it to pass.

Everything I went through as a child was connecting me to my calling and my purpose in life. Even though it did not feel good while going through it, it was all a part of God's perfect plan to push me toward my destiny. I realized that my tests and trials as a child were never about me, but they were about the tests and trials of other children that were like me. If my difficulties help bring hope and encouragement to someone that is going through something similar, then it was all worth it. I know what it feels like to want a better life, and be unable to change your present circumstances. I know what it feels like to have a dream on the inside that drives you. It is so real, that it will not let you quit.

I know my purpose in life is to help encourage hurting children. God has called me to serve as a bridge builder in their lives. He wants me to give them hope in spite of their current circumstances. My favorite scripture, Jeremiah 1:5, reminds me that before I was ever formed in my mother's belly, God knew me and approved me as His chosen instrument. This scripture confirms that no matter what is going on in your life, God has already set you apart as His chosen instrument. He had all of us on His mind before we were ever formed in our mother's womb. We cannot lose hope just because things may be difficult. We must keep pressing toward our destiny.

## AUTHOR BIOGRAPHY

**ShaQuita C. Gatewood** is a wife, mother, teacher, writer, public speaker, community leader, mentor, and founder and president of I Am Chosen, Inc. She has dedicated her life to helping children reach their fullest potential. She earned her Bachelor's degree from Tennessee State University in Elementary Education and a Master's degree in Educational Leadership. She is currently pursuing her Doctorate in Administrative Leadership.

In her career, she has taught in elementary schools and has served as a principal in a private Christian academy. Currently, she serves as the president of a non-profit organization for middle school girls, which she founded. It is called I Am Chosen, Inc. She was named the "Teacher of The Year" (2009-2010) at her local school, along with the honor of being one of eight semifinalists for the Douglas County School System top teacher's award.

ShaQuita's purpose in life is to serve as a bridge builder in the lives of children. It is her goal to help children reach their God-given potential, along with equipping them with the necessary tools and resources to overcome life challenges. During her spare time, ShaQuita enjoys spending time with her husband, Dr. Kendrick Gatewood, and their two children, Madison and Kaleb. She also volunteers throughout the community and within her local church.

ShaQuita embraces life and all that it has to offer. She is a woman of faith. Her faith has helped overcome many challenges in her life. She strives daily to live life with purpose, while making a positive and lasting impact in the lives of others.

## TESTIMONY 13

# *By Tifinie Capehart*

On Saturday September 3rd, 2011, I arrived at the wedding venue in Downtown Nashville with my 3 brides maids, clutching a note that my fiancé wrote to me:

> My Love,
>     The next time I see your beautiful smile, you will be presented to me, to love and cherish for the remainder of my natural life. I love you, today, and forever more.
>
> Love E.

I walked in the venue and saw both of our families smiling and laughing. They are ready to partake in a beautiful ceremony. I was so excited! I never really knew when this day would happen, or in what manner, but I knew that it would. I knew that I would marry someone who loved God and loved his family. Someone who could make me laugh, could relate to the brothers on the street as well as the brothers in the boardroom, and could dance – yes dance! So, here it was September 3rd, 2011, I was marrying the man that I'd asked God for. I was also marrying a man who God knew I needed – straight forward and honest, and steadfast in his beliefs and pursuits. It was a happy day.

My life wasn't always that way. There was a time, when I had no idea who was going to love me the way I needed to be loved. There was also a time, when I was made to feel less than deserving to be loved.

That situation only changed, when I was ready to hand over my love life to God.

Around 2005, I met someone who I thought was "the one". I was wrong. It wasn't all his fault; much of what I was put through I allowed:

"A man will only do to you what you allow him to do…" My mother

I didn't deserve to be lied to or cheated on for two years, but I didn't do much to stop it either. I would call it quits, but then find myself back in the 'relationship'. After a two-year merry-go-round and countless phone calls for advice with friends and my mother, I finally called it quits. The two-year charade left me emotionally tired, depressed, and defeated.

In early 2007, I began the process of healing and rebuilding by self-esteem. I began repeating a statement, which would become my personal motto, "Be Beautiful, Live Beautiful". I also began to pray, asking God to be my eyes, because I couldn't see what was good for me on my own. One evening, I confided in a close male friend, and he told me to just cry and pray – and I did. I stood in my closet one night, and cried and I prayed for my husband.

*"But when you pray, go into your room, close the door, and pray to your Father, who is unseen. Then your Father, who see what is done in secret will reward you."* – Matthew 6:6 (NIV)

After that prayer, I truly released it to God. In late 2007, I met the man that would become my husband.

I was formally introduced to him by my line sister at a networking event hosted by the Urban League Young Professionals. Immediately, I felt something that I'd never felt before. It was like an electric shock went through my body. And although it's cliché, it literally felt like butterflies. It wasn't the 'dang, he fine' butterflies, ladies, this was something different. I immediately felt connected to this man, whom I'd never met before.

"Tifinie meet Eric, he just proposed to his fiancé…." – My Line Sister

Well (insert expletive). The man's engaged. Okay, God, really?

"Yes my child….really…just be patient…" – God

Roughly six months, I had forgotten about my introduction and the 'feeling' I had, and continued rebuilding 'me'. My career was going well, I'd started a modeling hobby walking in local fashion shows, and was having fun meeting new people and making friends. I was becoming the woman I wanted to be. I was happy again.

I'd agreed to volunteer at a voter registration event, hosted by my line sister. The same woman who'd introduced me to Eric months earlier. She told me that he, too, would be volunteering and wanted to be paired with me. She also mentioned that he wanted to get out after having ended his engagement. Screeeeech...What!?

"I told you...just be patient..." - God

Eric and I talked and laughed through the night, and by the end of our shift, we had a date to the local symphony. Over the next several weeks, I would learn that he did rush into his previous engagement, and realized that it was not a good decision and broke it off. He would learn that I'd stopped casually dating, and was concentrating on 'getting my happy back' while releasing my love life to God. What we both discovered was that we were attracted to each other during our formal introduction, but it wasn't time for us to meet; it wasn't God's time. God knew that we both had to release some things before we would be able to move forward; and move forward we did.

Eric would help me trust again, and I would teach him patience. He was straightforward with me by explaining his intentions – marriage. And I would allow myself to be pursued and courted. During our courtship we had our ups and downs, and even considered breaking up a year into our dating relationship. However, we stayed prayerful and kept moving forward. We were both sure that this is what God had ordered.

"Be Beautiful, Live Beautiful." – Me

What I've learned and what I want to share with women, is that you have to allow yourself to be found. After I stopped looking with my own eyes and let God lead, I was able to see and accept the man that would become my husband. In addition, if someone is to find you, what will they find? Are you on the way to becoming the woman you want to be? Are you pursuing your own interests and desires or living for someone else? Make sure that you define your own happiness, that way you can bring someone into that space, and not rely on someone to create it for you. Lastly, when your mate does find you, will he find you preoccupied with things or people that can block your blessings? Finally, my last word of advice, eliminate relationships that don't edify you, preventing your mate from finding you.

My husband Eric and I, will celebrate two years September 3, 2013. We've truly enjoyed each other in our first year of marriage. We're still learning, and have a relationship just like any other couple. We get on each other's nerves from time to time, but I can't imagine anyone else in my life. He's truly my best friend and partner. I hope that this piece inspires other women to give their love life over to God, and exercise patience while waiting to be found.

"Be blessed." – Tifinie

## AUTHOR BIOGRAPHY

Tifinie Capehart is a Community Planner with the Metropolitan Nashville Planning Department's Community/Long-Range Planning Division. Tifinie is currently managing the community engagement portion of NashvilleNext – a process to create a plan for the future of Nashville for the next 25 years. Tifinie was the project manager for the 2010 North Nashville Community Plan Update, where over 300 stakeholders were engaged to develop land use policies to help guide growth and development for the community. Prior to the North Nashville Plan Update, Tifinie co-managed community planning efforts in Madison Tennessee, and the 12th Avenue South commercial district. Tifinie also co-managed the creation of the Community Character Manual (CCM), Nashville's land use policy guide, which is based on Transect planning principles and community character guided design principles. Tifinie currently serves as the Chair of the Nashville Food Policy Council, which is working to increase the availability of healthy and affordable food in Nashville/ Davidson County and in areas designated as food deserts. Tifinie holds a bachelor's degree in Engineering from Tennessee State University and a Masters of Planning Degree with an emphasis in Community Development from the University of Louisville.

Tifinie is married to Eric Capehart and resides in Nashville, Tennessee. Tifinie and Eric have spoken on local Christian Radio shows about relationships and dating, and believe that marriage is a ministry.

# By Alicia Igess

I moved to the city of Atlanta, Georgia to start my career as a hairstylist, and I became homeless in the process. No seriously, I lost all I had in a fire. No clients, no comb; I had nothing but my car. I did not come to the city with a built in clientele. Instead, I had to build a business and a home at the same time…from scratch. God's divine guidance, grace, and provision afforded me more success than I could have asked for or imagined. He can and is willing to do the same for you.

It is almost unbelievable to reflect on how I went from being a 22-year-old from Memphis, Tennessee, with nothing, to owning a thriving hair salon in Buckhead (Atlanta, Georgia). I now see celebrity clients in 10 states and three countries, and still find time to freelance on photo shoots for Ms. World International, RHOA Porsha Stewart and Gospel Today founder, Teresa Hairston, to name a few.

I love the beauty industry, and there are far too many talented stylists struggling to build a lucrative business. I literally get questions every day by stylists, salon owners, aspiring stylists and students on how I did it. How did I make this business work for me? If I can encourage one person to stay on track and follow her passion, I will have done my part, so do *not* give up.

I was born in the projects of Memphis, Tennessee. My mom was on public assistance my entire life. For some reason, God gave me the talent of doing hair. From the time I was three years old, I was playing in hair (my dolls, your dolls, my head, your head, whoever would allow me to practice). At the time, of course, I did not know I was practicing. I could sit around a salon all day long.

I literally started doing hair when I was 11 years old. I was finger waving for five dollars, and if you wanted it dried and lifted, I charged seven. Even at this point, I did not know I was practicing. All throughout junior high and high school, I had the opportunity to make money by doing hair. I meet people all the time that say, "I bet you knew the whole time you would do hair." I did not. It just so happens that I never stopped doing it.

I went on to college after high school, and I did hair in college. After I graduated from college, I finally decided to go to cosmetology school. That was the hardest thing in my life. I had a hard time because I thought I knew everything. But how many of you know that God's Word is true when it states that "pride goes before destruction, a haughty spirit before a fall" Proverbs 16:18 (NIV). Once I changed my mind-set, I was able to learn more of what was offered. I am so glad I listened.

If I could share anything with you, I would share these three principles:

## 1. Get focused.

You cannot succeed if you are not focused. What is it that you want to do or be? You do not have to know everything, just the one thing you are going to focus on right now. Habakkuk 2:2 (NIV) states *"Then the LORD replied: "Write down the revelation and make it plain on tablets so that a herald may run with it."* It may sound silly, but actually WRITE OUT your vision. Create a vision board and take steps everyday toward those goals. I'm a living witness that it works! God's ways and directions lead to success!

## 2. Get serious.

Stop playing with your future, and commit to being the best at what you do. Take classes, get a mentor, and get training.

Hebrews 12:11 NIV states that *"no discipline seems pleasant at the time, but painful; later on, however, it produces a harvest of righteousness and peace for those who have been trained by it."* It is so important to be disciplined fiscally and functionally. I've learned that another reason so many stylists struggle is due to a lack of work ethic, innovation and commitment. How many times do you walk into a salon and the stylist's hair is disheveled? Or the salon is dirty? Or, even worse, they look like they just woke up? If you do not take yourself seriously, how do you expect clients and potential clients to take you seriously? How you *show up* is vitally important to your success.

As a stylist in today's highly competitive market, it is important that you be more than a *good stylist*. Deuteronomy 8:18 states "*But remember the LORD your God, for it is He who gives you the ability to produce wealth, and so confirms His covenant, which He swore to your ancestors, as it is today*". (NIV) For me it was imperative that I not only recognize where my talents came from, but that I also continuously work to maintain, enhance and be a good steward of those talents.

There is a stylist on every corner, and YouTube is putting up tons of how-to videos daily. With the economy fluctuation, job security is not found in how good you do hair or the convenience of your salon location…God helped me to learn that it is about how you position your business. He guided me to the resources, education and industry knowledge that kept me from being in the position of having to chase clients for the rest of my life.

My ability to grow this business from nothing to greatness is certainly not solely due to my own efforts or actions. God certainly enabled me to have divine insight and divine innovation that shaped my business into what it is today. Romans 12:2 NIV clearly states "*Do not conform to the pattern of this world, but be transformed by the renewing of your mind. Then you will be able to test and approve what God's will is—his good, pleasing and perfect will.*" This is a commandment for innovation – never be a carbon copy of someone else. Never rest on your last level of success. It is imperative to renew yourself by committing to lifelong learning and continuous endeavors for improvement.

### 3. Get started.
Once you have a clear and focused vision, start taking yourself seriously, get started. Do not talk about it, do it.

No one has to say it for me. I know I am one hard-working sister, who believes absolutely anything is possible in life. This world is simply a playground where, as a small business owner, God allows me to create freedom, joy, and prosperity for myself, and those who come in contact with me. I have been blessed enough to experience how far determination and abilities can take you. I have been to places that I could never have imagined, and so can you.

I had lived in Atlanta, Georgia for less than three years when this "little ole country girl" from Memphis, Tennessee decided to open a hair salon. After a year of frustration with that property owner, I moved the business to Buckhead – a space we were in for nine years. During my time there, I trained more than 30 assistants, who are currently successful hair stylists in this beloved cosmetology industry. To follow up the success of the last nine years, my team and I are expanding our services to educate and train hair stylists at home as well as abroad. My dreams are becoming a reality, and yours can too.

How did I succeed? The reason is that I *never stopped and I never let fear control me.* Fear is the enemy of all entrepreneurs. Mark 5:36 (NIV) says *"Overhearing what they said, Jesus told them, "Don't be afraid; just believe."* There may come a time when you are the only one that believes in what God has shown you – never give up on the vision – never!

I never stopped believing I could do it, and took the correct steps to make it happen. *"I can do all things through Christ who strengthens me"* Philippians 4:13 NKJV. With God's help, I never stopped looking for solutions and I gathered an arsenal of advisors that could help me accomplish my dreams. *"Without the guidance of good leaders a nation falls. But many good advisers can save it."* Proverbs 11:14 NIRV. With prayer and grace, I found the strength to never give up on the dream of having freedom and job security and once that was achieved, I never lost sight of my visions or goals, or what my purpose on Earth really is.

II Timothy 1:7 (NIV) states that *"For the Spirit God gave us does not make us timid, but gives us power, love and self-discipline."* Don't allow fear to creep in and make you turn away from what you are called to do. I did not turn away from my God-given talents. God helped me to accept everything that was happening, to look to Him, and to find the strength to keep going. Allow yourself to do that, my friends. The strength and peace that God provides will take you to some amazing places. All you have to do is look to Him. Let Him bring you to your "Promised Land."

I challenge you to look to God's Word and find the same strength, the same power that He has placed within all of us. This power is divinely created, and when you tap into it, please believe me when I say, "There are no boundaries to what it can do."

## AUTHOR BIOGRAPHY

With over a decade of experience in hair design Alicia Igess is an accomplished stylist committed to her craft and the cultivation of new techniques. As the owner and founder of Urban Tangles Salon, she, along with her team, has experienced tremendous success in building an exclusive "referral-only" clientele consisting of many of the who's who of Atlanta.

Now that the time has come for Alicia to further evolve both the salon and her passion to have a greater impact in the beauty industry, growth for Alicia consists of expanding her brand and developing new talent to serve the next generation of future decision-makers, and for her to educate hair designers abroad. Her first course series will consist of color classes that focus on color dimension & skin tone blending.

In addition, Alicia is active in her Buckhead community both as a corporate and private citizen. She makes time to give back in time and resources to charitable organizations such as Buckhead Business Association, Junior League of Atlanta, and Delta Sigma Theta Sorority Incorporated.

*"Hair and educating others are my passion, helping people magnify their highest & best self is my gift." –Alicia Igess*

# By Nomalanga Mhlauli-Moses

## How I Re-Claimed My Body
## & My Life & How You Can Too

Roughly a year and a half ago, I walked across an international stage in a swimsuit, in-spite of having had two babies and, at one point, having weighed 200 pounds, even though I am only 5 feet 8 inches tall. The place was Orlando, FL and the event was Mrs. World 2011. Less than a year later, I did it again, and this time I was in a two-piece!

The reason why I am sharing a little bit of my story is that I want women to be able to take my story and use it to dispel the myths that they sometimes believe that lead to neglecting your health. I also want to inspire and encourage any woman who has a negative voice in her head that tells her that she CAN'T. And finally, I want us all to live happy (joyful) and healthy lives.

In 2009, I gave birth to a miracle baby boy who doctors told me may be born dead because of the severity of the gestational diabetes that affected my body at the time. When my son was born, I was also told that I should expect to have Type II diabetes soon after if I did not make changes to my lifestyle. I knew that my body was God's temple, that I had been bought with a price and that I needed to glorify the Lord with the vessel that He had blessed me with (1 Corinthians 6:19-20).

Here are a few tips to reclaiming your body and your life and accomplishing your goals:

## 1. Identify a WHY

For me, knowing that I may get diabetes was a big scare. Also, both my mother and my father are affected by the disease, as well as both of my grandmothers (one has already passed) and one of my siblings. But I needed yet another WHY to get me going and to stay motivated.

When I was younger, I had entered quite a few pageants and had even come in second at Miss Botswana 1997. (The winner, Mpule Kwelagobe, went on to become the first Black African to win the Miss Universe title, but I digress…). So, I decided to enter a beauty pageant, which had a swim wear competition. If walking across an international stage in a swimsuit was not going to motivate me, I don't know what would have!

For you, the WHY may be something else, but your WHY has to be something that will make you feel motivated and add a sense of urgency to you accomplishing your goal. Your WHY also has to go beyond YOU. For me, entering Mrs. Botswana and then Mrs. World was not just about me, my body and my diabetes; it was also about bringing awareness to various women's issues and pursuing a bigger platform from which to do that. It was as it says in 1 Corinthians 9:24-27 *"Do you not know that in a race all the runners run, but only one receives the prize? So run that you may obtain it. Every athlete exercises self-control in all things. They do it to receive a perishable wreath, but we an imperishable. So I do not run aimlessly; I do not box as one beating the air. But I discipline my body and keep it under control, lest after preaching to others I myself should be disqualified."* (ESV)

## 2. Do the WORK

December 2011: At Mrs. World

Once I had a WHY for making a change, I laid out a plan and got to WORK. I had to exercise more and become diligent about learning what to eat to get my body to not only look healthier and slimmer, but to also feel healthier. I started waking up at 4:30 am to get in some exercise. I also turned my lunch-break in to a 45 to 60 minute power-walk and in the evenings, as I watched one of my favorite TV shows, I would do it while riding my stationery bike. Remember, anything worth having is worth working for!

## 3. Choose your COMPANY wisely

I cannot stress how important it is to choose your company wisely. As it says in the Word of God, "bad *company corrupts good character*" 1 Corinthians 15:33 (NIV).

When I decided to enter the Mrs. World pageant, there were some family members and "friends" who told me it was "inappropriate for a married woman" to wear a swimsuit in public (side note: all 60 women in the pageant were married! ...hence the title MRS.). There were those who whispered behind my back, saying that I was not pretty enough or (fill in the blank) to enter a beauty pageant. Long story short, there were a lot of naysayers! BUT there were also those that showed up to encourage and affirm me.

One of my friends, who I happened to work with at the time, decided to join me in my lunch time walks and we enjoyed a lot of wonderful conversations and also encouraged, motivated and affirmed one another.

If you want to accomplish your goals in life, you have to get really good at discerning who to keep near and who to keep far. Negative people are not always bad people; in fact, naysayers can sometimes help you because they point out problems that you may not see, BUT more often than not, they are more harmful than helpful.

## 4. Help Others

I believe that one of the ways that you can be a successful human being is to make sure that you have the ability to take the focus off of yourself and place it on other people. There is a lot of joy in helping other people. As it states in Philippians 2:4 *"Let each of you look not only to his own interests, but also to the interests of others."* (ESV) You can help others by giving information, a word of encouragement, volunteering or whatever else you can think of. For me, helping others reach their goals also keeps me motivated and seeing other people succeed makes me joyful.

## 5. Be kind to yourself

Finally, be kind to yourself. After losing a lot of weight, I became temporarily ill due to the change in seasons and gained some of it back and for a while, I really beat myself up about it. Then I remembered that I have to be kind to myself. First of all, I have never returned to 200 pounds and second of all, I am not immune to set-backs, no one is. What I did was to continue to focus on my WHY and as I got better, the extra pounds started to slowly fall off. Be kind to yourself and also remember that there will be times when the old you tries to creep back. Remember your WHY and never give up. Isaiah 43:18-19 states it best when it says *"Remember not the former things, nor consider the things of old. Behold, I am doing a new thing; now it springs forth, do you not perceive it? I will make a way in the wilderness and rivers in the desert."* (ESV)

(By the way : my baby boy is a smart, loving and healthy four year old pre-schooler today and five years later, I am diabetes free).

## AUTHOR BIOGRAPHY

Nomalanga helps Black women thrive in their lives and careers. She is a Social Commentator, an Editor at Your Black World, Assistant Professor of Professional Studies and the reigning Mrs. Botswana.

# TESTIMONY 16

## By Anonymous

Have you ever been stuck in a job that made you feel hopeless? In this era that we live, most of us consider it a blessing just to have a job – any job – regardless of whether we truly feel fulfilled or not. But at one point in my life, I found myself so unfulfilled in with my occupation, that I cried out to the Lord for a change. I wanted more. I wasn't even sure what that "more" was but all I knew is that I wanted it.

The truth is that God wants us to enjoy our job, but the fact is most people don't. I was one of those people. A recent survey said 82% of the people say, "I hate my job." I could completely relate. Another survey done by the Princeton Research and Marketing Corporation of Princeton, New Jersey, said that between fifty and eighty percent of all Americans are in the wrong career because it doesn't match their gifts and abilities. How easy it is to find yourself in this predicament. I am a living witness that job frustration affects every other area of our lives.

I knew a change was coming, but forgot to heed the words "be careful what you pray for because you just might get it." I wanted to be free...free to truly choose my life. The choices get so murky sometimes. The lines of demarcation get blurred.

I knew that God wanted me to enjoy what I was doing. His word is clear - Ecclesiastes 5:18 states "*This is what I have observed to be good: that it is appropriate for people to eat, to drink and to find satisfaction in their toilsome labor...*" (NIV)

I had to make some hard decisions and I was caught up in the details of my choices. I was tired and drowning in misery...that societal misery that kept me harnessed to a job that I no longer enjoyed, "things" that no longer had any significant meaning to me, and a relationship that had long run its course.

I needed a break…a new direction. I needed more, and God gave me exactly that for which I had prayed. To some, it can appear that His *more* resulted in my *less*. But in actuality, God's more was absolutely perfect. I just had to execute the faith to step out into the unknown.

Rick Warren did a wonderful study on job satisfaction and summarized the requirements to obtain it: (1) having the right place, (2) the right perspective and (3) the right purpose.

Now I would be remise without noting that I fully recognized that whatever work that I did in life, I couldn't perform it as though I was actually performing the tasks for my boss. As it states in Colossians 3:23, *"whatever you do, work at it with all your heart, as working for the Lord, not for human masters."* (NIV)

I truly desired to find the right place for me. I was not prepared for the swiftness of my transition, nor fully prepared for the purposeful transformation that followed. When you make the decision to say "yes" to God's plan for your life, things always have a way of working out. After all, the Word says, *"Remember that the Lord will reward you for Christ is the real master you serve."* Colossians 3:24 (Good News).

Three years after transiting into a different position, life is still an adjustment, but my journey is filled with so much purpose through the things I choose to do. I am happier and calmer. I volunteer at least 20 percent of my time, talents, and treasure to my church. I now have time to not only smell the roses, but pick them, too. God has blessed me so much that there is not enough room on the page for my full testimony.

The icing on the cake is the wonderful, African-American company for which I now work. It is called JITA Enterprise, which stands for Jesus Is The Answer. Every day that I go to work, I cannot help but be reminded of His saving grace.

It amazes me when I consider God's infinite orchestration of my way out of "nowhere" to somewhere splendid. He certainly turned my ashes to beauty.

# TESTIMONY 17

## By Anonymous

But for having to give a testimony about forgiveness, and thereby having to speak in detail about the "test", I would have never discussed the following events. But I recognize that the enemy likes to utilize secrecy and sometimes silence as a means to further deceive us and rob us from victorious living.

Have you ever had to fight to hold on to a blessing that God has given you? Surely, I am not the only one. Whether you obtained admission into a university, and then had to overcome numerous obstacles in order to graduate; or whether you finally landed that dream job, and then had to deal with the difficulty of office politics —many of us have been in a situation where we had to take a stand for Christ and hold fast to the promise that He gave us.

There comes a point in life when you have to resolve that you will not let go of God's blessings, you will not compromise God's standards, and you will hold fast to the purpose and assignment that the Lord has for you. Often, present in these types of situations is a person or persons being used to attack, withhold, or pervert the very blessing that God has for you. You will be required to fully forgive them in order to be truly free. I once read somewhere that the first to apologize is the bravest; the first to forgive is the strongest; and the first to learn from it and move on is the happiest. I believe this to be absolutely true. Allow me to tell you my story of how God gave me beauty for ashes through the power of forgiveness.

# The Calling - Purpose

Before I jump into what I have to share, I want to tell you the reason I compete in pageants. Prior to entering my very first pageant competition back in 2007, I had the opportunity to speak to a group of young girls about setting goals, boosting self-worth, and making wise decisions for their lives. I remember going back to my office feeling elated. I knew that encouraging women of all ages to live victoriously was certainly one of the many things that God had called me to do.

I remember sitting in my office as I said a quiet prayer. I prayed that God would allow me to be positioned to combat the attack on the self-esteem and confidence levels of women and youth. I prayed He would grant me a position, which would allow me to speak to women and youth about His goodness and to tell them how they could have confidence in Him and His design for their lives. I prayed for the opportunity to express to them the truth about the unwavering love He has for them.

God's answer was pageantry. I didn't even want to do a pageant when God first whispered it. I was a grown, 30- year-old woman. I was an accomplished lawyer after all. I was an adjunct professor of business law and in-house counsel to one of the largest corporations in the nation. Why did I need to parade around in a swimsuit and subject myself to the judgment of others? This was my first response because of my flesh. In my mind, I said to myself, "Don't do that. You do not need to prove to anyone that you are pretty. That is beneath you. You are far too intelligent for that. What will your legal colleagues think? What will the church think? What if they don't understand?" My thoughts continued to race through my head, "What are you going to do? You have been told that if you don't wear a two-piece swimsuit and show a lot of skin you cannot win. You don't stand a chance. These women have been at this for years – you can't just start at this now and think you have a chance – no way." Those were the negative thoughts the enemy whispered to me, but, as usual, he was totally wrong. Just as God Himself once posed a rhetorical question, "Behold, I am the LORD, the God of all flesh. Is there anything too hard for Me?" (Jeremiah 32:27 KJV).

I began to study the book of Esther (the first historical account of a beauty pageant can be found in this wonderful book of the Bible) and realized that each of us is called to do something that we are uniquely designed to do. As it states in 1 Peter 4:10 (NIV) "Each of you should use whatever gift you have received to serve others, as faithful stewards of God's grace in its various forms." For me, it is pageantry with purpose. God has equipped and called me to a ministry of helping youth and women have higher levels of self-worth through the knowledge of who they are in Christ. That is one of the assignments on which the Lord wants me to do. What's your gift? What's your ministry?

At one point in time, I asked God to allow me to have a major "door opening" pageant title. You see, there is a difference when Miss Apple Pie United requests a speaking engagement as opposed to Miss Universe or Miss America. The bigger the title, the more opportunities one has to reach people. I didn't need another accomplishment or accolade for my own enjoyment. No, this journey through pageantry was not at all about me. It was about that calling that I had answered several years prior. I still held on to my assignment from God, and I still desired to encourage others to live victoriously through Christ and obedience to God's Word. I knew that pageantry was the vehicle that He had whispered to me to utilize in order to accomplish this purpose.

You see, the devil has no problem putting forth images and idols to deceive young girls and women into thinking that they must compromise themselves and their walk with Christ in order to *win* in life. Nothing could be further from the truth. When I prayed that God would give me more opportunities to encourage and equip the Bride, in preparation for the return of Christ, and when I heard the whisper of pageantry as the vehicle, I said, "Okay God, let's do it." Even though I had never thought of entering a pageant before in my life, I knew that all things were possible with Christ. "I can do all things through Christ which strengtheneth me" (Philippians 4:13 KJV).

# The Journey - Divine

It was a beautiful night. It had been a long journey, but I was here on the final evening of the weeklong pageant competition. It was a tough, yet quite enjoyable international pageant competition. The title I was competing for was honorable, prestigious, and most importantly, it was a "door opener" title that would allow me to talk about where confidence should truly come from – from the Lord.

I prepared for several months – working out, talking to my pageant coaches, preparing my competition wardrobe, and making arrangements for my family while I would be away. I remember reflecting on one of my favorite pageant prep scriptures: "For I know the thoughts that I think toward you, says the LORD, thoughts of peace and not of evil, to give you a future and a hope" (Jeremiah 29:11 NKJV). There is much that goes into competing at this level. The queries set forth in the paperwork that the judges would receive required the contestants to provide a very detailed and inclusive marketing plan and community service history. I made sure I provided a comprehensive purpose-driven marketing plan concerning what I would do if I had the title. Fast forward to the actual competition, all the contestants arrived and had a great time getting to know each other. To this day, some of the women I met there are still good friends of mine.

During the week, I experienced some very strange obstacles. While going for an early morning run on the beach, I began to just focus on God's goodness and praise Him. Then I got a text from my friend, who came with me to support me during the competition. She informed me that there was a sewage flowing up from the toilet in our room, and it was filling our entire room. Had she not been there, and had she not been guided by the Lord to think quickly, my entire pageant wardrobe would have been destroyed. The water was so high that it soaked through my luggage that was on the floor. If she had not had the presence of mind to move my gowns, the bottom of my competition attire would have been covered in sewage water. Some of my items were damaged, but nothing of vital importance. I lost my intended competition swimsuit in the flood, but praise God I had a spare. God had me covered, and I remained focused on why I was there. I knew God was going to use this title to open doors for me to help others, and more importantly, to help women and young girls know that they are all royalty in God's kingdom.

When it came time for us to compete, we all became very focused. The interviews with the judges were all videotaped, and some of the ladies felt they were very intense, although I rather enjoyed it. Interview has always been my strong suit. I had a pageant coach who called to ask me some interview questions as a warm up prior to my interview. The questions we practiced turned out to be the exact questions presented to me by the judges during my interview. Now, how divine was that? God also used my other pageant coach who sacrificially tutored me via Skype at one o'clock in the morning. We worked on my stage presentation (walk routine for swimsuit, evening gown, and fashion wear). God will send help in your time of need, according to His promise. "Let us therefore come boldly unto the throne of grace, that we may obtain mercy, and find grace to help in time of need" (Hebrews 4:16 KJV).

Preliminary night was fun for me. On stage, we were competing in swimsuit (yikes), evening gown (my favorite) and fashion wear (fun). After preliminaries, the ladies with the top scores were required to do it all over again, substituting interview for an on-stage Q/A. Contrary to popular belief, it is actually very challenging to win a pageant competition at this level – but through Christ all things are indeed possible.

For some reason, the night of the finals, I began to feel a great sense of anxiety and nervousness right before I went out on stage. I closed my eyes and did my normal method of calming my nerves. When I stood at the edge of the entry point on stage, I remember feeling sick. I literally wanted to throw up. I was overcome with nervousness. I had to stop, pray, and remember that Jesus was right there with me. I recited 2 Timothy 1:7, "For God hath not given us the spirit of fear; but of power, and of love, and of a sound mind." (KJV). God calmed my nerves. I was ready. I had made wardrobe selections that I felt would be pleasing to the Lord and still competitive. You can be fashionable and faithful in your commitment to glorifying the Lord in all that you do. "And whatsoever ye do, do [it] heartily, as to the Lord, and not unto men" (Colossians 3:23 KJV).

# The Victory – To God Be the Glory!

Through it all, God allowed me to make it to the final cut. I was there, standing on stage with many fantastic and dynamic women. Each of us accomplished, committed, beautiful, and passionate about the causes we desired to champion for the upcoming year. They called out the fourth runner up, the third runner up, then the second runner up – and I was still standing. They then called the first runner up. I was still standing there. I could only imagine what my mother, father, husband, friends, and church family were thinking while watching this live via internet back home. At last, they announced it. The winner of this year's international title was – ME!

They called my name and time stood still for a moment. Could this be? All that I had gone through to get to this point – finally it happened. I stood there in shock. I did the typical hands on the side of the face – "oh my goodness, I won" – facial expression. As they placed the amazing crown on my head and draped the sash across my chest, I looked out at the judges, and some of them were moved to tears, too. It was a glorious moment.

# The Work Begins...

After I won, the real work began. I was excited and ready to hit the ground running. Every contestant that year had been informed by the staff, director, and previous queen that whoever was chosen as the winner would need to be a self-starter. They wanted someone who did not need a lot of handholding. They were looking for someone with connections and appearances already set up so that, as soon as they were crowned, they could get to work promoting not only their platform or charity, but also the pageant system as a whole. Oh, was I the right one for the job. I did just that. In a matter of 40 days, I had made about 10 appearances. Keep in mind that, unlike pageant queens that compete at the teen or Miss level, in the Ms./Mrs. pageant level, 10 appearances is more than some queens make during their entire reign. I was determined to make the most of this opportunity with which God had blessed me with.

## Distractions, Obstacles, and Offense: The Battle Begins

One would assume that my testimony ends here. God gave me the victory to go forth and fulfill the assignment that He had for me. He had prepared me for this moment, and it was so perfect it seemed almost too good to be true. Well...

## Changes and Confusion...

A few months into my reign, I began to notice some strange changes. The name of the title that I won was changing. Remember, as I mentioned earlier, the actual name of the title that you are given is a prize in and of itself. It was what I had prayed for, and God had answered that prayer. Doors were opening, and I was busy about my Father's business. I kept looking at the title displayed on the sash that I wore; then I looked at the new name on the website and was truly confused. The name of the title on the website changed, then the name of the title on Facebook changed, and then the name of the title on Twitter changed. At first, I thought perhaps it was a typo; but, based on the level of professionalism that I had encountered from the staff of the system, I surmised that it was no mistake. No one said a word to me about any changes to the title. Up to this point, I made several appearances for various events and charities for months utilizing the pageant title that they bestowed upon me. I finally called and sent an email inquiring about the name change. What resulted from that inquiry would prove to be the foundation for one of the most challenging seasons in my life.

Eventually I received a call from three representatives from the organization who proceeded to tell me that the pageant corporation decided to change the company's name and my title – in the middle of my reign. They also proceeded to give me a rationale for the change in name which, in my opinion, was legally unsound, ambiguous, and illusory. The rationale that they put forth simply left me with more questions than answers. Being well-versed in the areas of trademark and contract law, the conversation raised numerous red flags. It was clear to me that I was legally entitled to every prize that was promised at the time of my crowning, and that included the title I received. In my opinion, I had not been provided with a legally legitimate reason that would require me to willingly forfeit any of the prizes that were promised.

Now, one could pause and say, "Who cares, right? What's in a name really?" Some women would love to have any pageant title- whether they were Miss America or Miss Paperbag! So what if it is odd to change a pageant queen's title from that which she was crowned in the middle of her reign? And so what if the new title is totally different? Initially I thought that surely they could have waited to make this change until my reign was over, they could change the name of their company as they deemed necessary and could simply allow me to crown the upcoming queen under the new title the following year. But no, they were making the change to the title that they crowned me under during my reign, no questions asked, done deal!

To a certain extent, I would agree with the initial "so what" reaction. I mean really, who cares what they call the title? A pageant title is a pageant title, right? Well ... not so much -or at least not to some. To be totally transparent, the new title that they created was one which I would not have signed up to compete for. It was like going from having the title of Miss America to Miss Wonderful Lady Idol United or going from having the title of Miss World to Miss Grand Woman Role-Model Unlimited. It was a non-traditional pageant title, and while it may be perfectly fine for others, it was not what I signed up for. It certainly wasn't what I prayed for, and it wasn't what God promised or gave me. In addition, there was a part to the new title that really conflicted with my spirit and contained a word that was the synonym for the word 'idol'. It all really did not sit well with me. I wasn't keen on wearing a title that called me an "idol". I wasn't here for anyone to worship or idolize. God had placed ministering to young girls and women through pageantry on my heart and I just wanted to be obedient and sensitive to that. I did not want young girls looking up to me as an idol.

From a practical standpoint, I knew (and was later proven to be correct) that it would be substantially harder to pursue and obtain engagements for book signings and public speaking events under the new title. Remember, there is a difference between trying to obtain speaking engagements as Ms. Wonderful Lady Idol United or Miss Grand Woman Role-Model Unlimited versus having the more respectable title of Miss Universe, Miss World or Miss America – or any title that is familiar to the general public and traditional enough that people at least recognize it when they hear it. When others learned of the new title, most people would ask me what it meant and would seem puzzled. Many in the pageant industry, including some that had been affiliated with this particular pageant system in the past, stated that the new title lacked dignity and was adding to the "toddlers & tiaras" image that the general public has of pageantry because the new title was so strange. It was as if the enemy couldn't keep me from receiving my blessing of winning a prestigious title, so he was now attempting to pervert it and make a mockery of it. I recalled the scripture which states "be sober, be vigilant; because your adversary the devil, as a roaring lion, walketh about, seeking whom he may devour" (1 Peter 5:8 KJV). He could not stop me from winning the competition, so he was trying to turn something that was great into an area of shame by making a mockery of it. He was also attempting to use the staff of the system to lie about the reason behind the change in order to get me distracted from the purpose God had for me in the first place.

## Deception and Distractions ...

While my discontentment with the new title could have been overcome; that certainly was not the most concerning issue. I was extremely concerned about actual reason for the change – and rightfully so. I attempted again to get clarity with regard to the real reason for the name change. I called one of the staff members who proceeded to yell at me that I should "take on the new title or give up the crown" and then hung up the phone in my face. Yet again, their behavior raised several red flags and I developed a growing concern. I decided to conduct some research on the US Patent and Trademark Office website; and I discovered that the title I was given hadn't received trademark protection. In fact such trademark application was denied a year before I was crowned.

I remember thinking why on earth would a pageant organization go forward to crown someone with a title that had been denied trademark protection? In the denial document from the US Patent and Trademark Office attorney that is public record, it makes it pretty clear that the pageant title that they gave me would infringe on the trademark rights of other pageant organizations. Why not just be forthcoming about this? I wondered why the name of the title hadn't been changed prior to the competition. How on earth could they have possibly not known about this – they filed the application – they received notice of the denial – so how and why did this happen? I was crowned a certain title and I had appearance requirements to fulfill as the reigning queen. Yet each time I wore the sash, I was wearing a title that had no trademark protection and could potentially infringe upon the trademark rights of others. Why on earth would anyone allow this to happen? Why wasn't I told? Why was this fact not included in the rationale that was given for the change to the title to begin with? This was very unsettling for me. I remember praying to God and saying "Hey, I didn't sign up for this! All I wanted to do was sign up for a pageant and all I did was win – I didn't sign up for potential legal battles and for so much drama – Lord what is going on"? Looking back on it, with prior knowledge of the forthcoming change, I would have chosen a different system, but that choice was taken away from me.

Shortly thereafter, I received a contract containing the new title and other shocking new contractual terms. Naturally, I switched into lawyer mode and responded by providing them with a corrected contract that reflected what, in my opinion and based on the documents they previously provided, should have been the proper contractual terms. After sending the revised contract, I received a letter in which the pageant organization attempted to dethrone me.

Yes, you read that correctly – they attempted to take the title from me! The "de-throne letter" stated that they viewed my actions of not accepting the new title within 10 days as disrespectful and that they had decided to take away my title. I would no longer be considered to be affiliated with the organization "in any shape, form, or fashion whatsoever." I read the letter, and I just sat there. I thought, "Surely not. They can't be serious. Not the crown and opportunity that God had given me. What is happening here?" I said to myself, "I'm just trying to be about my Father's business. All I did was enter a competition and legitimately win. All I wanted to know was the basis for the change and how much liability they could have possibly subjected me to!" I later discovered that they proceeded to speak negatively to several people and attempted to bring shame upon me. It was frustrating but most of all it was hurtful. I considered these people my friends. I had known one person in particular for years. But God in His word promises "instead of your shame you will receive a double portion, and instead of disgrace you will rejoice in your inheritance. And so you will inherit a double portion in your land, and everlasting joy will be yours." Isaiah 61:7 (NIV). If you have ever had someone to try and speak against you behind your back or to bring shame upon you – this scripture is for you! God will keep His word – you will receive a double portion! God has a lot of things that He wants you to inherit in your life.

A double portion I received indeed!!! What ensued was a bit of a legal battle, and when all the dust settled, God gave me a double portion for my pain. Not only did I keep my title, I also received a full indemnification from the company for any liability I could face and I kept the right to receive every prize I was owed. I also had a right to receive settlement payments. I never had to wear the sash with the new title until I arrived at the pageant competition the following year to crown my successor. God gave me the year He had promised and I remained focused on what He called me to do. I made over 30 appearances in over 7 countries – all to the credit of the Lord.

# Offense and Anger... Sin Not! ...

While I had a very successful and fulfilling year with regard to the ministry work I was able to perform through the Lord's help, it was also a very challenging year. After all of the negotiations and settlement terms were reached, the communications with the pageant staff for the rest of my reign were acrimonious at best. During my entire reign, I was given the silent treatment unless communication was absolutely necessary. I was the face of their organization, I made numerous appearances all year; but for months, I was blocked from the organization's Facebook group and my email address was blocked from sending any correspondence to the very organization whose site bore my face on it. Some of the prizes owed to me never manifested.

On one occasion the organization attempted to mail some of the prizes to me, but when the package was returned to them because of their failure to address the customs and duty fees, the package went unclaimed by their office for so long that it was sent to the national unclaimed mail center and the contents were set to be auctioned off. For four months I inquired about the location of the package and was told that they were not aware of its location. They finally provided the tracking details that I had been requesting for almost four months and I was able to retrieve the package within 48 hours. Even the simplest of communications and tasks became knotty. I found the entire experience extremely disrespectful and offensive. It was beyond disappointing.

I was frustrated, offended, and angry. I was angry that this situation momentarily placed a dark cloud on what should have been one of the happiest times of any pageant winner's career. It made me angry that they were not forthcoming with the truth and then tried to dethrone me for addressing the issues. It made me angry that no one in the organization ever apologized for how I was treated. Anger also came from the fact that I had to keep smiling, and I could not tell anyone what was really happening. As it says in Proverbs 16:28, "A perverse man sows strife, and a whisperer separates close friends". (AMP) I was doing all I could to not speak of this situation outside of my immediate family that had to know. Yet others in the pageant community were telling me how they would slander my name on many occasions. I had to keep smiling when I wanted to cry at times. No one could know just how disrespectful the situation truly was. I had to deflect my answers to questions regarding how my reign was going from the public and from other women who were contemplating whether or not to compete in the same pageant system. I remember reflecting on Proverbs 26:20 (NIV), "For lack of wood the fire goes out, and where there is no whisper, contention ceases".

I was angry, disappointed, hurt, and saddened. It was also awkward and at times dramatic when I had to go and crown my successor the following year. I hadn't seen or spoken to some of the pageant system's staff in over 10 months. It was a tough year – I remained the queen for the organization – but I had to obtain my own PR help with appearances in support of charitable causes. Still to this very day, new contestants, judges, and others in the pageant industry share how the staff of the organization continues to speak ill of me. I won't bore or belabor the subject matter concerning the other offensive acts that transpired during my reign.

Have you ever been deceived or had information withheld from you in an attempt to cover up the truth? Have you ever worked really hard for something and had the enemy ever worked through others to turn a beautiful blessing or situation into something stressful, disrespectful and disconcerting? Have you ever had to take a stand, perhaps even take legal action, to enforce what is right and just? Rest assured that God is not operational in the midst of lies and deceit. He does not change His mind, and He is not the author of confusion – the devil is, however.

It is so easy to forgive others for things that are minor in your sight. Maybe someone was rude or did something that was somewhat offensive; perhaps they lied or deceived you, but you don't have to really interact with them that much. Perhaps someone did something to you, but he or she apologized.

But, what if someone deceives you repeatedly? What if someone intentionally lies to you and the result of the lie impacts your purpose, mission, or places you in harm's way? What if they never apologize for their wrong actions? What if they not only fail to apologize, but they continue to disrespect you? What if you have to continue to work alongside people who are so prideful that they will never admit their wrongdoing? What if you have not seen justice served fully for the wrongdoing? What if you really have to walk out the scripture of "loving your enemies" and being "kind to those who are unkind to you"? How can you do this? The answer, of course, is in God's Word.

## The Power of Forgiveness

We are not strong enough to forgive others on our own. For me, I can firmly say that this year-long experience offense affected something that I held very near and dear. It was personal. It was hurtful, and it was continuous; but the Bible does not say to forgive when the person stops the offensive or unjust act. It does not say to forgive after they have apologized or repented. In the Lord's prayer, it says "forgive us our trespasses, as we forgive those who trespass against us..." but there is no mention of the trespasser "repenting". No, we are commanded in Luke 6:27 (NIV) to "... Love your enemies, do good to those who hate you, bless those who curse you, pray for those who mistreat you". Without a doubt, we are commanded to forgive – end of discussion. I am a living witness that you CAN forgive those who continuously offend, hurt, deceive, mishandle, or mistreat you! With Christ, it can be done! Forgiveness is not just a tool, or a defense, it can be a mighty weapon!

In fact, what motivated me the most to start the healing process of forgiveness while in this situation was realizing the fact that failing to do so could actually result in distancing myself from God. It took a while for me to push past the disappointment, offense and the hurt, but ultimately I went to the Bible in search of how I could possibly begin to forgive the people that were unrepentant—continuously causing me hurt and offense. You cannot dwell on or develop a "someone must pay" attitude, because someone already did pay—Christ died on the cross for your sins and for the very acts that caused you hurt, offense, or pain at the hands of another.

So where do we start?

Do you know what? It all started with prayer and a decision. You must pray that God will give you the strength and the heart to forgive. I decided first that I would follow God's Word regardless of my emotions. I would give God a *yes* to His commandment. God commands that we forgive so I decided I would forgive and keep on forgiving. Again, in the Lord's Prayer it says, "Forgive us our trespasses as we forgive those who trespass against us." Why is forgiveness so important? Why is it essential to our own well-being and our spiritual walk? I learned that there are a few reasons why.

Most importantly for me is the fact that unforgiveness hampers our own relationship with God. Failing to forgive is an act of disobedience—plain and simple. As with any act of disobedience, it retards our relationship with the Father. It also leads to pent-up resentment toward the person who has sinned against us. We cannot love God and hate our fellow man, as stated in Matthew 22:39, "....Thou shalt love thy neighbor as thyself." (KJV) Hanging on to unforgiveness, that keeps us in a state that is other than loving, can dampen our spiritual walk.

Secondly, unforgiveness can lead to internal emotional stress. There is bondage in not being forgiving. And the one in bondage is the one who won't forgive the other. During the time that all of this initially transpired, I was so angry, upset, and had such unrest that my skin began to break out. It was caused by pent-up frustration from the months that it took to negotiate a settlement agreement that would govern my reigning year. Each negotiation act made me more and more upset. I was angry that they lied, but I was also unforgiving, and this unforgiveness continued to tie me to the unjust actions against me. I had to leave it to God. You cannot get over it or move on with your life until you forgive the person and put the consequences of their actions into God's hands. That was hard for me as a lawyer because the injustice of it all hit hard with me, but I had to realize that the bad things that have been done to us in the past cannot be changed. Having grudges does not help anyone, and it does not hurt the people whom we hold the grudge against. They have sinned against us and moved on with their lives. Giving them over to God allows us to also detach ourselves from the situation and move on. Resentment and bottled-up anger just lead to stress, which is extremely unhealthy, both physically and emotionally.

I won't pretend that it was an overnight process, but the more I started to pray for them and asked God to help me to forgive, the more my heart began to open up for God to come in and heal me. I remember my pageant coach sent me a link to a song by Mathew West called *Forgiveness*. Again, God will send you a word right when you need it. My coach was one of the few people, outside of my family, whom I had spoken to about the situation. I listened to the song and the lyrics rang so true for me. It ministered to my soul. Part of the lyrics state, "Forgiveness is anger's worst enemy. Even when the jury and the judge, say you gotta right to hold a grudge, it's the whisper in your ear saying set it free—forgiveness."

Oh, how I needed to hear those words. Then I researched the actual history of the song and learned how a mother forgave the young man who killed her daughter while driving drunk. I found out how they went on to join together on a campaign against drunk driving, but more importantly they started a ministry regarding forgiveness. I remember realizing how powerful the act of forgiveness truly is. If this mother could forgive, then surely I could, too. We all need to remember that forgiving someone is showing them mercy that they do not deserve, just as God, through sending His Son to die for our sins, gave us mercy that we didn't deserve. You must give the same mercy that you so readily received from God. You can't wait for the other person to apologize. That may never happen. Forgiveness is not actually about the wrongdoer; forgiveness is really between the Lord and us. God makes it clear that vengeance is not ours to act upon—it belongs to Him. "Dearly beloved, avenge not yourselves, but [rather] give place unto wrath: for it is written, Vengeance [is] mine; I will repay, saith the Lord" (Romans 12:19 KJV).

I can truly say that I am over it – I have no ill will towards anyone. I pray that this experience allowed us all to grow and that the future will be great for everyone involved. From that situation I now have a testimony to share with others and prayerfully it can set others free through the power of forgiveness and help inspire others to live a life of integrity, honesty, and kindness.

## What I Learned...

1. Hold fast to what God has given you and never let go. The enemy will try to come in and pervert or steal what God has done in your life. Make the decision never to let go. Pray that God reveals all deception, lies, and tricks of the enemy. Fast and pray so that you can have clarity on how to handle the situation. You cannot control the actions of others, but you can control your reaction to their decisions. Take the limits off God. No matter what something seems like in the natural, God will fulfill every promise He has made for us. If He said it, it will come to pass. Circle around the promise!

2. Pain is a necessary part of the birthing process. In order for there to be expansion in your life and for new things to come forth, there must be labor and contractions. They are painful but necessary. I wouldn't have known my own strength. These types of situations push you into your destiny. I would have stopped competing and would have never had the content for this book and a great reality docu-series, but God has much greater on the horizon. God can truly take a painful situation and turn it around for your benefit. He will "prepare a table before me in the presence of my enemies" Psalms 23:5 (NIV), and truly I am living witness that "...in all things God works for the good of those who love Him who have been called according to His purpose".

3. Forgive is not a noun – it is a verb. It is actionable. It is about making a choice and taking action. Moving on from the place of hurt is not only freeing – it is POWERFUL. When we forgive we offer mercy—mercy that isn't earned, but freely given. Pray for those who hurt you because hurt people do hurtful things. They need deliverance, mercy, grace, and a second chance. Forgiving others is not just about the other person, it is about you. It is about your

ability to really be Christ-like, even when you have been hurt. It is about you having been wronged and still doing what is right. It is a beautiful thing to forgive because it is divine. God gives that ability. It is only through Him that we are strong enough to do such a thing. Character and integrity are really shown in what you do when no one is looking. It is about what is in your heart.

We have to choose to forgive and keep on choosing it. When we do this, we cut the ties to the emotional hurts and can begin to heal. Forgiving someone really starts the process of alleviating the pain that we have held onto, due to the offense or hurt that the other person has caused us. When you start to forgive that person, the anger and pain will start to lessen and will eventually go away. Moving on is the key. I obtained a different international title after that trying year was over. It was even more prestigious than the former, and had it not been for me moving on, I would have missed that blessing. Ask me today if I am angry, and I will say absolutely not. I have moved on from glory to glory.

One exercise that I find extremely helpful is to make a list of EVERY SINGLE act or instance that you can recall that you feel that you were wronged, and forgiveness is needed. After you have completed your list(s), go outside, with your list and a match(es), pray again that God will provide you with the strength and grace to forgive them, then light on fire and offer it, as it were, as a burnt offering to God. I mean BURN IT! Let it go. Release it! Doing this physical act will give you a release that can't even be put into words!

4.   Don't become distracted. Focus on the positive through the pain. I can't reiterate how important it is to remember that God will see you through a difficult season the same way He has seen you through other obstacles in your past. In that same vein, it is also important to make a list of all the positive things that are happening in your life. A minister at a church I attended in law school once said that some of our problems in life are like quarters to the sun. He explained that in life, a quarter is only a few inches big; but if you take your arm, hold the quarter up in to the sky and align it with the sun, you can actually make the quarter appear to be the same size or bigger

than the sun. It is all about perspective. If you bring the quarter down and hold it eye level, keeping it in its rightful perspective, you will see the quarter in its intended and rightful size. Taken out of perspective and placed above your head, the quarter looks bigger than what it is. It looks as big, if not bigger, than the sun. This is what many of us do with our problems. We don't keep them in the right perspective and they become bigger than the Son – seemingly larger than Jesus. The problem becomes so overwhelming that we inadvertently say to ourselves, this situation is beyond God's ability to fix it. We may not verbally say those words, but we certainly behave that way.

5. What's in a name? A rose by any other name would smell as sweet right? Wrong. In Exodus chapter 5, we see where Adam goes about naming the animals. When you name something, you give it essence. This is why the Nazi's took the Jews' names away and gave them numbers – to take away the essence of who they are. Watch the title and labels you allow others to give you. Be sure that the titles or names that you take on or answer to are in line with your purpose and who God says you are. Your name is to remind you of your purpose. Never let anyone change the essence of who you are! It is so important for you to have an accurate assessment of who you are. Because sometimes, if you let someone change your name, you will let someone change your purpose. Who are you? What do you stand for? In what level of integrity are you operating? Will you compromise to please others? Will you cover up the truth and participate in a lie for the sake of succeeding? What does it profit a man to gain the whole world and lose his soul?

6. Seek wise counsel. "Plans fail for lack of counsel, but with many advisers they succeed" (Proverbs 15:22 NIV). Watch the friends that are around you and the advice that you take in. "Iron sharpeneth iron; so a man sharpeneth the countenance of his friend" (Proverbs 27:17 KJV). I was reminded by so many wonderful advisors and friends about the importance of forgiveness and what it truly means to forgive. Equally important, I was also reminded what forgiveness is NOT!

- Forgiveness is not trusting, forgiveness is granted freely, trust is earned;
- Forgiveness is not excusing the other party;
- Forgiveness is not avoiding or abandoning justice;
- Forgiveness is not ignoring consequences
- Forgiveness is not reconciliation;
- Forgiveness is not approving or diminishing the sin (Christ died for ALL sin, so don't dishonor the death of Jesus and what was accomplished on the cross by approving or diminishing sin – it all matters so much that it required Christ to die for it!);
- Forgiveness is not waiting on an apology;
- Forgiveness is not enabling the sin to continue; and
- Forgiveness is not ceasing to feel the pain.

7. Praying the Word of God and seeking guidance from the Holy Spirit can fortify you and provide the strength you need to overcome any obstacle. Get a routine of Bible study. Make it a part of your life.

## Beauty for Ashes: Moving Onward and Upward

There is a distinct beauty to forgiveness because it enables you to move on to better things. It opens up the opportunity for God to continue to bless you as you take your focus off the offense and place it back on God. That is exactly how it played out in my personal experience. Once I quit dwelling in the hurt and offense, I prayed and received God's healing as well as other amazing blessings.

As I prayed for continued healing, I whispered my desire to God that my pageant career would not end on this kind of note. I did not want my future ministry to be associated with a title that is not in keeping with my values. However, to be blunt, I was very tired at that time. Most major competitions require a 7-10 day commitment, and I just didn't know if I had the energy to do it. It is not only hard on me; it takes a toll on my husband and children as well when I am gone for that length of time.

I expressed the desires of my heart to the Lord in some very specific ways. I prayed that I could be part of a major pageant and only have to compete for a few days, even though that is simply not realistic. Amazingly, the Lord has opened up the opportunity for me to be personally invited to compete in a different well-known international pageant. So many doors have begun to open having obtained the regional title through this system. That has been such a major answer to prayer, but it gets even better. Due to the fact that I had to go and crown my successor for the title that I held at that time, I permitted to represent my region and join the national competition for the last three days of the week long competition – how specific is that answer to prayer?

While at the competition, God answered yet another prayer. When I received the new regional pageant title, I prayed for nothing more than to go to the national competition and win one of the silver sash title awards. God answered my prayer again! I was awarded on stage the wonderful honor of receiving a great new silver sash award/title with this new system! What an honor and blessings – and it means so much to me because it came from those who matter—it was a result of the outpouring of millions of on-line voters who took the time out to not only vote, but to leave written words explaining how they felt about me and how I had affected their lives or communities. God allowed me to get a glimpse of the footprint or legacy I have started to leave and gave me flowers while I was still living. It was amazing! I also have a wonderful relationship with the staff and director of that system and I had more speaking engagement, modeling, acting, and pageant opportunities pouring my way on a daily basis than ever before! I've been signed to a serious acting management agency and I would have never even thought of pursuing that dream had it not been for the encouragement and inspiration that I received from so many which poured out of this experience. It is truly a blessing. Again, God will give you a double portion as it states in Isaiah 61:7. "Delight thyself also in the LORD; and he shall give thee the desires of thine heart" (Psalm 37:4 KJV).

Without a doubt, God is faithful to those who trust in Him. God helped me to focus on Him, His perfect will for my life, and the ministry He had blessed with me instead of on the wrong actions and attitudes of others. Through that experience, I have learned much about the power of forgiveness and how to truly love others as Christ loves us. When you trust and obey the Lord, no matter what the circumstances, He will move you from glory to glory. "But we all, with unveiled face, beholding as in a mirror the glory of the Lord, are being transformed into the same image from glory to glory, just as by the Spirit of the Lord" (2 Corinthians 3:18 NKJV).

The thing that you are going through today is just temporary and it is subject to change. God wants you to rejoice. If you will let go of the past, He will move you forward. The plans that He has for you are good and not evil, to give you hope and a future! Jeremiah 29:11 (NIV). Your best ministry comes out of the places where you bled. How much hope can I give to others by sharing how God healed me through the power of forgiveness from the pain of being lied to, rejected, deceived, and mistreated. If you don't quit and you keep saying 'Yes' to Jesus, no matter what man says God will fulfill every promise in your life. God will indeed give you joy for your shame, and beauty for your ashes.

This book is brought to you by
Happy To Be You Ministries Inc.,
Media Division

To find out more,
please visit:

www.happy2bu.org

or

www.juanitaingram.com

Made in the USA
Middletown, DE
10 February 2022